Companion to the Solicitors' Code of Conduct 2007

SECOND EDITION

COMPANION TO THE SOLICITORS' CODE OF CONDUCT 2007

SECOND EDITION

Peter Camp

The Law Society

© The Law Society 2009

ISBN–13: 978–1–85328–803–6

Published in 2009 by the Law Society
113 Chancery Lane, London WC2A 1PL

Typeset by Columns Design Ltd, Reading
Printed by TJ International Ltd, Padstow, Cornwall

The paper used for the text pages of this book is FSC certified. FSC (the Forest Stewardship Council) is an international network to promote responsible management of the world's forests.

FSC

Mixed Sources

Product group from well-managed
forests and other controlled sources

Cert no. SA-COC-1530
www.fsc.org
© 1996 Forest Stewardship Council

Contents

Preface

The Solicitors' Code of Conduct 2007 (the Code) came into force on 1 July 2007. Since that date a number of minor amendments have been made to both the rules and the guidance notes. However, on 31 March 2009 the Code rules and guidance notes were amended substantially to allow for the partial implementation of the Legal Services Act 2007. Notably, the Code has been amended to cover the introduction of legal disciplinary practices and entity-based regulation.

The second edition of this Companion identifies all the main changes made to the Code since 1 July 2007. Like the first edition, it is not intended to provide 'stand-alone' guidance but is designed to be read and used in conjunction with the Code (written by the Solicitors Regulation Authority and last published by the Law Society in June 2009).

The structure of this Companion remains the same as it was for the first edition: after the Introduction, the chapter numbers and headings correspond with the rule numbers and headings in the Code. Changes made in both the rules and guidance are highlighted in each chapter.

I have quoted from the rules and guidance but the views expressed in the Companion are mine, and only where the context allows should these views be taken as being endorsed by either the Solicitors Regulation Authority or the Law Society.

Peter Camp
June 2009

Abbreviations

1999 Code	Solicitors' Costs Information and Client Care Code 1999
2009 Amendment Rules	Solicitors' Code of Conduct (LDPs and Firm Based Regulation) Amendment Rules 2009
ABS	alternative business structure
ADR	alternative dispute resolution
CCBE	Council of the Bars and Law Societies of Europe
Code	Solicitors' Code of Conduct 2007
CPD	continuing professional development
LCS	Legal Complaints Service
LDP	legal disciplinary practice
LLP	limited liability partnership
LSB	Legal Services Board
OLC	Office for Legal Complaints
REL	registered European lawyer
RFL	registered foreign lawyer
SEAL	Solicitors' Estate Agency Limited
SPR 1990	Solicitors' Practice Rules 1990
SRA	Solicitors Regulation Authority

The Solicitors' Code of Conduct 2007 (as amended by the Solicitors' Code of Conduct (LDPs and Firm Based Regulation) Amendment Rules 2009)

BACKGROUND

On 1 July 2007, the Solicitors' Code of Conduct 2007 (the Code) came into force. Since the commencement date there have been a number of minor amendments to the guidance notes (which do not form part of the Code). These are covered, in context, in the appropriate chapters of this Companion.

However, in October 2007 the Legal Services Act 2007 was given Royal Assent. This Act makes significant changes to the way in which legal services are provided and regulated in England and Wales. Five major issues are covered by the Act:

- The creation of the Legal Services Board (LSB), which will supervise the regulation of legal services by approved regulators, e.g. the Solicitors Regulation Authority (SRA), the Bar Standards Board and the Council for Licensed Conveyancers.
- The introduction of 'firm-wide' regulation. In order to provide reserved legal services (as defined) to members of the public both the individual providing or supervising those services and the firm must be regulated.
- The introduction of legal disciplinary practices (LDPs). For example, regulated firms are capable of having, as principals, solicitors and registered overseas lawyers (as has been the case for some time) together with other defined 'lawyers' such as barristers, licensed conveyancers and legal executives. In addition up to 25 per cent of the principals in a firm can be non-lawyers – i.e. persons approved by the SRA as suitable persons to be involved in the provision of legal services.
- The introduction of the Office for Legal Complaints (OLC) – a new independent ombudsman service to deal with all consumer complaints about legal services. The OLC will cover the work of all lawyers and will deal with redress – not with regulation.

- The introduction of alternative business structures (ABSs) allowing for external ownership of law firms – e.g. by banks, supermarkets or listed plcs. ABSs will also be capable of providing a multi-disciplinary practice – combining the provision of a number of distinct professional services under one roof.

By the end of 2008, the Chair and members of the LSB had been appointed but the LSB is not expected to commence its supervisory role until early 2010. By late 2010 it is hoped that the OLC will be fully operational. The first ABSs are expected to be licensed to provide legal services in late 2011.

However, the introduction of firm-wide regulation and LDPs is not dependent upon a fully operational LSB or OLC. The changes requiring firm-wide regulation and the introduction of LDPs (including practices with non-lawyer principals) have been made by the SRA by way of amendments to the Code. The amendments were made by the Solicitors' Code of Conduct (LDPs and Firm Based Regulation) Amendment Rules 2009 (referred to in this Companion as the 2009 Amendment Rules) and came into force on 31 March 2009.

The Code as originally issued in July 2007 contained the Solicitors' Recognised Bodies Regulations 2007. These regulations have been replaced, in the light of firm-wide regulation, by the SRA Recognised Bodies Regulations 2009. New regulations (SRA Practising Regulations 2009) have been issued dealing with applications for practising certificates, applications to be a recognised sole practitioner, the register of solicitors with practising certificates and the register of European lawyers, and foreign lawyers.

The amendments to the Code are covered in depth in this Companion.

As with the first edition of the Code, the amended version does not contain all the professional rules issued by the SRA and applicable to the profession. The provisions relating to accounts, indemnity insurance, financial services and the compensation fund remain in force as separate rules, although significant amendments have been made to these rules as a result of the introduction of firm-wide regulation and LDPs. Specifically these are (with amendment rules shown where appropriate):

(a) Solicitors' Accounts Rules 1998 (as amended by the Solicitors' Accounts (Legal Services Act) Amendment Rules 2009)
(b) Solicitors' Indemnity Insurance Rules 2008 (as amended by the Solicitors' Indemnity Insurance (Amendment) Rules 2009)
(c) Solicitors' Indemnity (Enactment) Rules 2007
(d) Solicitors' Financial Services (Scope) Rules 2001 (as amended by the Solicitors' Financial Services (Scope) Amendment Rules 2009)
(e) Solicitors' Financial Services (Conduct of Business) Rules 2001
(f) Solicitors' Compensation Fund Rules 2009
(g) Solicitors' Compensation Fund (Foreign Lawyers' Contributions) Rules 1991

Guidance on the above rules will not be found in the Code (other than where any of these rules impact on rules contained in the Code) and these rules are not covered in this Companion.

FORMAT OF THE CODE (AS AMENDED)

The Code comprises three elements:

- **The core duties.** The six core duties (contained in rule 1) are fundamental rules. A breach may ultimately result in the imposition of sanctions.
- **The rules.** The rules (rules 2–25) arise from the core duties and give more detail on the minimum standards required to comply with the core duties. A breach may result in the imposition of sanctions.
- **The guidance.** Guidance is provided after each of the rules. The guidance is not mandatory and does not technically form part of the Code. (The guidance is referred to throughout this Companion by note number.)

APPLICATION OF THE CODE (RULE 23)

The Legal Services Act 2007 introduces a new term, 'manager', which is used extensively in the amended Code. 'Manager' is defined (rule 24) as:

(a) a partner in a partnership;
(b) a member of a limited liability partnership (LLP); or
(c) a director of a company.

Significant changes have been made to rule 23 detailing the application of the Code. The Code applies to you if you are practising from offices in England and Wales and you are a solicitor or a registered European lawyer (REL) (including recognised sole practitioners practising as solicitors or RELs), or a recognised body (all practices other than recognised sole practitioners must now be recognised bodies). (An REL is an individual registered with the Solicitors Regulation Authority under regulation 17 of the European Communities (Lawyer's Practice) Regulations 2000 (SI 2000/1119) (Establishment Directive Regulations).)

The Code also applies to any other person who is a manager or employee of a recognised body or the employee of a recognised sole practitioner practising from an office in England and Wales. Rule 24 (Interpretation) defines 'practice from an office' to include practice from an office at which you are based. Consequently the Code applies to in-house practice as well as private practice (see in particular rule 13 (In-house practice, etc.)).

Unlike the earlier version of the Code, the rules contained in the Code now have direct application to employees (and managers) who are not solicitors. The SRA can impose sanctions directly on non-solicitor employees and managers. 'Employees' for these purposes are defined as those employed as

3

a director of a company or those engaged under a contract of service or a contract for services with a firm (rule 24). The SRA has issued guidance on 'New duties for employees and firms', available at **www.sra.org.uk/code-of-conduct/guidance/2405.article**.

Note that some of the rules apply to conduct outside professional practice. For example, 1.06 and 10.01 apply specifically to behaviour outside practice (see note 10 to rule 1 and note 1 to rule 10 – Chapter 1 and Chapter 10) and undertakings are binding where given by a solicitor or REL outside the course of practice, but as a solicitor or REL (see Chapter 10).

The Code also applies to any registered foreign lawyer (RFL) practising from offices in England and Wales as an employee of a recognised sole practitioner; a manager, employee, owner or director of a recognised body; or as a manager, member or owner of a body corporate which is a manager, member or owner of a recognised body. (An RFL is an individual registered with the SRA under the Courts and Legal Services Act 1990, s.89.)

The Code applies to practice from an office outside England and Wales to the extent noted in rule 15 (Overseas practice) – see below Chapter 15.

One new feature of LDPs introduced by the Legal Services Act 2007 is that solicitors, RELs and RFLs may choose to practise through a firm (an LDP) that is regulated by a body other than the SRA provided that the work they do is restricted to work of the sort authorised by the firm's regulator. For example, a solicitor who undertakes conveyancing work could become a manager or an employee in a firm of licensed conveyancers which was authorised by the Council for Licensed Conveyancers.

In these circumstances, the Code would have limited application to solicitors, RELs and RFLs practising as such. Only rule 23 (Application of these rules) and rules 1 (Core duties), 12 (Framework of practice), 20 (Rights and obligations of practice), 21 (Separate businesses) and 24 (Interpretation) would apply to solicitors, RELs and RFLs practising through an authorised non-SRA firm.

CHAPTER 1

Core duties

INTRODUCTION

Rule 1 contains six core duties. These 'form an overarching framework within which the more detailed and context-specific rules in the rest of the Code can be understood' (see note 2(b) of the guidance to rule 1). A breach of rule 1 may result in disciplinary proceedings against the solicitor, recognised body, REL, RFL or non-solicitor employee or manager.

The core duties can assist in situations not specifically covered by the other rules of the Code (see note 2(c)).

Core duty 1.06 (Public confidence) applies to behaviour within or outside professional practice (see note 10 of the guidance to rule 1). This applies equally to overseas activities outside professional practice undertaken by, for example, solicitors, RELs or RFLs (see rule 15(1)(b)(i)).

SCOPE

The core duties apply to:

- solicitors or RELs practising from offices in England and Wales (including recognised sole practitioners practising as solicitors or RELs);
- recognised bodies (all practices other than recognised sole practitioners must now be recognised bodies);
- any other person who is a manager or employee of a recognised body or the employee of a recognised sole practitioner practising from offices in England and Wales;
- any RFL practising from offices in England and Wales as an employee of a recognised sole practitioner; a manager, employee, owner or director of a recognised body; or as a manager, member or owner of a body corporate which is a manager, member or owner of a recognised body;
- overseas practice (see rule 15);
- solicitors, RELs or RFLs practising through a non-SRA authorised firm.

CORE DUTY 1 – JUSTICE AND THE RULE OF LAW (1.01)

This duty refers to 'Justice and the rule of law'. This covers the duty owed to the court which is expanded in rule 11. However, the duty also covers relations with third parties dealt with on behalf of a client (expanded by rule 10).

CORE DUTY 2 – INTEGRITY (1.02)

This duty requires those bound by the Code to act with integrity.

CORE DUTY 3 – INDEPENDENCE (1.03)

This duty requires those bound by the Code not to allow their independence to be compromised. The guidance note to 1.03 (note 7) refers to rule 3 (Conflict of interests) and rule 9 (Referrals of business) as being relevant in the context of independence. However, significant examples of what situations might put independence at risk have been added to note 7 by the 2009 Amendment Rules. These are:

(a) finance agreements/loans to your firm with particular strings attached;
(b) finance arrangements which suggest dependency upon an outside body, such as could, at that body's discretion, effectively put your firm out of business;
(c) contractual conditions in agreements with referrers of business or funders which effectively cede control of your firm to the outside body;
(d) granting options to purchase your interest in your firm for nominal value;
(e) allowing a third party access to confidential information concerning your clients;
(f) a relationship with an outside body which is not at arm's length, and/or which suggests that your firm is more akin to a part of or subsidiary of that body, rather than an independent law firm;
(g) fee sharing arrangements which go beyond what is allowed under rule 8.02;
(h) any arrangement for a third party to fund legal actions which lays constraints on the conduct of the matter which go beyond the legitimate interests of a funder.

CORE DUTY 4 – BEST INTERESTS OF CLIENTS (1.04)

This duty requires those bound by the Code to act in the best interests of each client. The guidance note to 1.04 (note 8) refers to rule 4 (Confidentiality and disclosure), rule 3 (Conflict of interests) and 10.01 (Not taking unfair advantage).

CORE DUTY 5 – STANDARD OF SERVICE (1.05)

This duty requires those bound by the Code to provide a good standard of service to their clients. The guidance (note 9) refers to the exercise of competence, skill and diligence. The rule imposes 'conduct' obligations (and therefore, potentially, disciplinary action) on top of the requirements at law to provide services with reasonable skill and care. Isolated or minor breaches of this duty will not necessarily give rise to the imposition of sanctions.

CORE DUTY 6 – PUBLIC CONFIDENCE (1.06)

This duty requires those bound by the Code not to behave in a way that is likely to diminish the trust the public places in them or in the legal profession and the guidance (note 10) makes it clear that any behaviour within or outside professional practice that undermines the trust can give rise to a breach of this duty. The word 'legal' has been inserted before the word 'profession' in 1.06 by the 2009 Amendment Rules. This has extended the duty in 1.06 to cover behaviour that is likely to diminish the trust the public places in any profession:

- whose members are solicitors, barristers or advocates of the UK;
- whose members are authorised to practise by an approved regulator other than the SRA;
- which is a legal profession of an Establishment Directive state other than the UK;
- which is a legal profession approved or recognised by the SRA.

Under the Legal Services Act 2007 the following are approved regulators:

- the Law Society (acting through its independent regulatory body, the SRA);
- the Bar Council (acting through the Bar Standards Board);
- the Master of Faculties;
- the Institute of Legal Executives;
- the Council for Licensed Conveyancers;
- the Chartered Institute of Patent Attorneys;
- the Institute of Trade Mark Attorneys; and
- the Association of Law Costs Draftsmen.

CONCLUSION

The 2009 Amendment Rules do not really make any significant changes to the obligations of a solicitor, recognised body, REL or RFL in relation to the core duties in rule 1. However, the scope of the obligations is extended to cover all employees and all managers (whether they are lawyers or not). Practitioners should note the examples given in note 7 of situations that might put independence at risk.

The amendment to 1.06 (Public confidence) means that this core duty can be breached by activities that diminish the trust the public places in an extended number of professions.

CHAPTER 2

Client relations

INTRODUCTION

Rule 2 covers a number of miscellaneous topics relating to client relations. The following topics are covered by rule 2:

- Taking on clients
- Client care
- Information about the cost
- Contingency fees
- Complaints handling
- Commissions
- Limitation of civil liability by contract

The Code introduced some subtle changes to the requirements on client care and on information about costs. Practitioners will need to keep under review their internal procedures on these topics to ensure proper compliance.

SCOPE

Rule 2 applies (where the context provides) to:

- solicitors or RELs practising from offices in England and Wales (including recognised sole practitioners practising as solicitors or RELs);
- recognised bodies (all practices other than recognised sole practitioners must now be recognised bodies);
- any other person who is a manager or employee of a recognised body or the employee of a recognised sole practitioner practising from offices in England and Wales;
- any RFL practising from offices in England and Wales as an employee of a recognised sole practitioner; a manager, employee, owner or director of a recognised body; or as a manager, member or owner of a body corporate which is a manager, member or owner of a recognised body.

Rule 2 does not apply to overseas practice but note that 15.02(2)–(4) imposes certain client relation rules on overseas practice. These are:

- an obligation to pay client commissions (15.02(2));
- a prohibition on excluding liability by contract but an ability to limit civil liability subject to a minimum level and other conditions (15.02(3));
- restrictions on contingency fees (15.02(4)).

Rule 2 does not apply to solicitors, RELs or RFLs practising through or employed by a non-SRA authorised firm.

TAKING ON CLIENTS (2.01)

Rule 2.01 confirms that there is, generally, freedom to decide whether or not to accept instructions to act for a particular client. The guidance notes (note 4) provide examples of where this freedom is subject to restrictions.

The rule also lists circumstances where there must be a refusal to accept instructions or where, if you are already acting, you must cease to act for a client. Again the guidance notes (note 6) expand on these circumstances.

Guidance note 7 provides that, as a matter of good practice, you should not act for a client who has instructed another firm to act on the same matter unless the other firm agrees. The note, however, confirms that a second opinion can be given without breaching good practice, providing you have sufficient information to do so.

Rule 2.01(1)(c) deals with third party instructions. The Code requires you not to proceed where instructions are given by someone other than the client (or by only one client on behalf of others in a joint matter) without checking that all clients agree with the instructions given. Although there is no requirement that the client's agreement is recorded in writing, seeking written confirmation must be good practice and provides evidence of the requirement that all clients have agreed with the instructions.

A small amendment was made to the guidance in July 2007. Guidance note 3 was amended to remind practitioners that the retainer is a contractual relationship and subject to legal considerations. It states that you should be sure as to who is your client if you provide services to a third party.

Rule 2.01(2) confirms that you must not cease acting for a client except for good reason and on reasonable notice. Notes 8–11 to rule 2 expand on the duty not to cease acting without reasonable cause.

The Code concentrates upon conduct issues and generally does not give guidance on legal issues (except where there is a close relationship between conduct and the law). In the context of litigation services, practitioners should refer to the Solicitors Act 1974, s.65 which provides a good reason to terminate a contentious business retainer where a client has (after reasonable notice) failed to put the solicitor in funds for work done or to be done.

Further, note 11 to rule 2 refers to the client's paperwork following the termination of a retainer. It briefly deals with the exercise of a lien over the client's papers in order to secure costs. The note refers practitioners to *Cordery on Solicitors* for further guidance.

CLIENT CARE (2.02)

Rule 2.02 covers the client care obligations formerly set out in the Solicitors' Costs Information and Client Care Code 1999 (1999 Code).

Rule 2.02(1) imposes four obligations on practitioners. Practitioners must:

(a) identify clearly the client's objectives in relation to the work to be done for the client;

(b) give the client a clear explanation of the issues involved and the options available to the client;

(c) agree with the client the next steps to be taken; and

(d) keep the client informed of progress, unless otherwise agreed.

Consequently, on taking instructions, it will be necessary to ensure that the client's objectives are clearly identified, that the client is given a clear explanation of the options open to the client and that an agreement is reached with the client as to the next steps to be taken.

Many firms have, historically, satisfied these requirements – their inclusion in the Code requires all firms to consider the information given to clients at the outset of a retainer.

In addition to the obligations in 2.02(1), further and additional information must be given as a result of 2.02(2). This rule applies at the outset and as necessary during the course of the matter. Consequently its provisions will not necessarily be satisfied simply by the inclusion of the information in the firm's engagement letter. An ongoing obligation to supply this information applies. By reference to 2.02(2), you must:

(a) agree an appropriate level of service;

(b) explain your responsibilities;

(c) explain the client's responsibilities;

(d) ensure that the client is given, in writing, the name and status of the person dealing with the matter and the name of the person responsible for its overall supervision; and

(e) explain any limitations or conditions resulting from your relationship with a third party (for example a funder, fee sharer or introducer) which affect the steps you can take on the client's behalf.

The guidance to 2.02 (note 12) makes it clear that the purpose of the rule is to set out the type of information that must normally be given to the client (both before and during a retainer). It adds that the information must be provided in a clear and readily accessible form. Practitioners must keep under review their engagement letters and other means of providing information to clients in the light of these provisions.

Rule 2.02(3) states that if you can demonstrate that it was inappropriate in the circumstances to meet some or all of these requirements, there will be no breach of 2.02.

There are useful guidance notes (guidance note number shown in brackets) covering:

- the level of service (14);
- the options available to the client (15);
- the limitations or conditions arising from a relationship with a third party (16 and 17);
- the status of the person dealing with the matter (19);
- the person responsible for the overall supervision of the matter (21);
- circumstances where it would be inappropriate to provide any or all or the information (22);
- the receipt of instructions from someone other than your client (24).

INFORMATION ABOUT THE COST (2.03)

Rule 2.03 covers the costs information requirements formerly contained in the 1999 Code. The basic requirement is to be found in 2.03(1) which requires you to give clients the best information possible about the likely overall cost of the matter. This obligation applies at the outset and also, where necessary, as the matter progresses. Specifically you must:

(a) advise the client of the basis and terms of your charges;
(b) advise the client if charging rates are to be increased;
(c) advise the client of likely payments which you or your client may need to make to others;
(d) discuss with the client how the client will pay, in particular:
   (i) whether the client may be eligible and should apply for public funding; and
   (ii) whether the client's own costs are covered by insurance or may be paid by someone else such as an employer or trade union;
(e) advise the client that there are circumstances where you may be entitled to exercise a lien for unpaid costs;
(f) advise the client of their potential liability for any other party's costs; and
(g) discuss with the client whether their liability for another party's costs may be covered by existing insurance or whether specially purchased insurance may be obtained.

The 1999 Code provided examples of information which would satisfy the requirement to provide 'best information possible'. This is not repeated in rule 2.03 of the Code, nor is it contained in the guidance notes in the same depth. Note 36 provides limited guidance. However, that is not to say the examples in the 1999 Code should be ignored – these may be relevant in appropriate cases. For example, the 1999 Code (para. 4(c)) stated that giving 'the best information possible' includes:

(i) agreeing a fixed fee; or
(ii) giving a realistic estimate; or
(iii) giving a forecast within a possible range of costs; or
(iv) explaining to the client the reasons why it is not possible to fix, or give a realistic estimate or forecast of, the overall costs, and giving instead the best information possible about the cost of the next stage of the matter.

The guidance to 2.03 states that you are free (usually) to negotiate the cost and the method of payment with clients and it will not normally be necessary for clients to be separately advised (note 31). However, where unusual methods are proposed separate advice may be necessary (note 34 gives the example of receiving shares in a new company instead of costs).

The requirement in 2.03(1) includes the obligation to advise the client that there are circumstances where you may be entitled to exercise a lien for unpaid costs. Practitioners should consider including this statement in their standard engagement letter in order to comply with the rule. In the context of termination of the client retainer, note 11 gives limited guidance on the exercise of a lien over the client's papers for unpaid costs. As a matter of law (see *Cordery on Solicitors*) solicitors are entitled to exercise a lien; as a matter of conduct they must advise the client of that right at the outset of a retainer.

The requirements of 2.03(1)(f) and (g) are, again, simplified statements of obligations previously contained in the 1999 Code. Much of the greater detail contained in the 1999 Code is still relevant and may be required information as a result of the requirement to give 'best information possible'.

By way of illustration, 2.03(1)(f) states that you must 'advise the client of their potential liability for any other party's costs'. The 1999 Code stated that a solicitor should explain to a client the potential liability for the costs of any other party, including:

- the probability that the client will have to pay the opponent's costs as well as the client's own costs if the case is lost;
- the fact that even if the client wins, the opponent may not be ordered to pay or be capable of paying the full amount of the client's costs; and
- the fact that if the opponent is legally aided the client may not recover costs, even if successful.

Rule 2.03(2) covers the position where a firm is acting for a client under a conditional fee agreement and requires clients to be told the circumstances in which they 'may be liable for your costs and whether you will seek payment of these from the client, if entitled to do so'.

Additional information must be given to publicly funded clients (2.03(3)). This includes a requirement that clients are told of the circumstances in which they may be liable for your costs and advised of the effect of the statutory charge.

The remaining provisions of 2.03 are as follows:

- where fees are to be shared with a charity, a requirement to disclose the name of the charity (2.03(4));
- information concerning costs must be clear and confirmed in writing (2.03(5));
- a requirement to discuss cost benefit and risk (2.03(6));

- a statement that there will be no breach of 2.03 if it can be demonstrated that it would be inappropriate in the circumstances to meet all or some of the requirements (2.03(7)).

Finally, it should be noted that neither the Code nor the guidance notes deal with the form a bill can take; final or interim bills; when they can be delivered; and when and how a firm can sue on a bill. Some guidance can be found in *Cordery on Solicitors*.

CONTINGENCY FEES (2.04)

Rule 2.04 contains restrictions on the use of contingency fees. A contingency fee, for these purposes, is defined in rule 24 as 'any sum (whether fixed, or calculated either as a percentage of the proceeds or otherwise) payable only in the event of success'.

Rule 2.04(1) prohibits contingency fees for work done in prosecuting or defending any contentious proceedings before a court of England and Wales, a British court martial or an arbitrator where the seat of arbitration is in England and Wales unless such a fee is permitted by statute or common law. Rule 2.04(2) prohibits contingency fees in contentious proceedings before an overseas court or arbitrator except where permitted (see below). The rule is helpful since it expands on the definition of contentious proceedings (contained in the Solicitors Act 1974, s.87) by referring to the type of proceedings giving rise to contentious proceedings. The prohibition does not apply to non-contentious matters. For example, most tribunal proceedings are non-contentious proceedings (unless the tribunal has the status of a High Court, e.g. the Employment Appeal Tribunal) and in consequence it might be possible to charge a contingency fee in respect of such proceedings.

The guidance notes (note 44) confirm that conditional fee arrangements are a form of statutory, permitted contingency fees. The notes (note 45) also make it clear that contingency fees are permitted in non-contentious matters but to be enforceable they should be contained in a non-contentious business agreement (these are agreements (defined in the Solicitors Act 1974, s.57) which must be in writing and signed by the person (or his agent) to be bound by it). Non-contentious matters cover dispute resolution retainers up to the commencement of proceedings. Consequently, a contingency fee may be charged in an otherwise contentious matter provided legal proceedings are not started (see note 46).

Rule 2.04(2) allows for contingency fees to be charged in contentious proceedings before a foreign court or arbitrator where a lawyer of that jurisdiction would be permitted to charge on that basis.

COMPLAINTS HANDLING (2.05)

Rule 2.05 covers matters relating to complaints handling. As originally drafted in 2007, the rule's scope was restricted to a 'principal in a firm'. The 2009 Amendment Rules have extended the scope of 2.05 to recognised bodies, managers of recognised bodies or recognised sole practitioners. The text of the rule states:

(1) If you are a recognised body, a manager of a recognised body or a recognised sole practitioner, you must ensure:

    (a) that the firm has a written complaints procedure and that complaints are handled promptly, fairly and effectively in accordance with it;

    (b) that the client is told, in writing, at the outset:

        (i) that, in the event of a problem, the client is entitled to complain; and

        (ii) to whom the client should complain;

    (c) that the client is given a copy of the complaints procedure on request; and

    (d) that once a complaint has been made, the person complaining is told in writing:

        (i) how the complaint will be handled; and

        (ii) within what timescales they will be given an initial and/or substantive response.

(2) If you can demonstrate that it was inappropriate in the circumstances to meet some or all of these requirements, you will not breach 2.05.

(3) You must not charge your client for the cost of handling a complaint.

As a result of 2.05, managers and sole practitioners must regularly review their complaints procedures and as a matter of obligation must ensure their procedures comply with the following:

- The client must be given the information required by the rule in writing.
- The client must be told of his or her entitlement to complain in the event of a problem.
- In the event of a complaint, the person complaining must be told in writing how the complaint will be handled and within what timescales an initial and/or substantive response will be given.
- No charge can be made for the cost of handling a complaint.

Note 2 to rule 2 confirms that a material breach of 2.05 may provide evidence of inadequate professional services.

COMMISSIONS (2.06)

Rule 2.06 mirrors the legal position which prevents a solicitor making a secret profit from the solicitor–client relationship (note 52). Rule 2.06 imposes an obligation on recognised bodies, managers of recognised bodies or recognised sole practitioners to pay commission of more than £20 to the client unless the client has given informed consent to the firm to retain it. As originally drafted and issued in 2007, 2.06 applied to 'principals in a firm'. It now applies to equally to the firm (i.e. the recognised body).

The rule requires the client to be told the amount or, if the precise amount is not known, an approximate amount or how the commission is to be calculated before giving consent to the retention of the commission. It clearly is good practice both to notify the client in writing and to obtain the client's consent to retention in writing.

The guidance notes provide further information regarding commission, including:

- a definition of commission (note 53);
- a requirement that you must make it clear that the client can withhold their consent and, if so, the commission will belong to the client when received (note 56);
- a requirement that commission can only be retained if the arrangement is in the client's best interests either because it is used to offset a bill of costs or, for example, it is retained in lieu of costs which are not billed (note 57);
- a statement that it cannot be in the best interests of the client for commission to be retained as a gift (note 58);
- the position where the commission is materially different from the estimate (note 58(c));
- the requirements of the Solicitors' Accounts Rules 1998 regarding commission (note 61); and
- a warning regarding commission received in the context of financial services (note 63). Many firms will avoid the need for authorisation from the Financial Services Authority under the Financial Services and Markets Act 2000 either by showing that an appropriate exclusion will apply (leading to the conclusion that no authorisation is required because the firm is not undertaking regulated activities) or by showing that the firm is undertaking exempt regulated activities (i.e. activities which are exempt from the need for authorisation). A condition which applies to a major exclusion (where arrangements are made with or through an authorised person) and a condition relating to exempt regulated activities both require all commission to be accounted to the client. Unlike rule 2.06, these conditions do not include a £20 de minimis figure – to use the exclusion and/or the exemption all commission must be accounted.

LIMITATION OF CIVIL LIABILITY BY CONTRACT (2.07)

The basic obligation in 2.07 applies to recognised bodies, managers of recognised bodies or recognised sole practitioners. The rule prohibits the exclusion or attempted exclusion by contract of all liability to clients. As originally drafted and issued in 2007, 2.07 applied to 'principals in a firm'. It now applies to equally to the firm itself (i.e. the recognised body).

However, civil liability may be limited provided such limitation is not below the minimum level of cover required by the Solicitors' Indemnity Insurance Rules (currently £2m for non-incorporated bodies; £3m for most incorporated practices (i.e. LLPs and companies)).

Rule 2.07 requires any such limitation to be brought to the client's attention and the limitation must be in writing.

The notes to 2.07 (notes 64–72) give extensive guidance on the limitation of liability. Note 65 indicates that it would be inappropriate to include the limitation in terms of business without specifically drawing the client's attention to it.

Notes also deal with the position relating to trusts (notes 66 and 67) and notes 68–72 give guidance on the position at law.

CONCLUSION

The 2009 Amendment Rules do not really make any significant changes to the obligations contained in rule 2. However, the scope of many of the obligations is extended to cover all employees and all managers (whether they are lawyers or not). Where the old rule applied only to 'principals in firms' (notably 2.05, 2.06 and 2.07) the new rule applies to recognised bodies, managers of recognised bodies or recognised sole practitioners.

CHAPTER 3

Conflict of interests

INTRODUCTION

Rule 3 sets out the requirements relating to conflict of interest. The following topics are covered in rule 3:

- Duty not to act
- Exceptions to duty not to act
- Conflict when already acting
- Accepting gifts from clients
- Public office or appointment leading to conflict
- Alternative dispute resolution (ADR)
- Acting for seller and buyer in conveyancing, property selling and mortgage related services
- Acting for lender and borrower in conveyancing transactions

At the time of writing, the SRA has issued a consultation paper on amendments to rule 3 (with responses required by 31 March 2009). Brief details of these proposed changes appear in this chapter.

SCOPE

Rule 3 applies (where the context provides) to:

- solicitors or RELs practising from offices in England and Wales (including recognised sole practitioners practising as solicitors or RELs);
- recognised bodies (all practices other than recognised sole practitioners must now be recognised bodies);
- any other person who is a manager or employee of a recognised body or the employee of a recognised sole practitioner practising from offices in England and Wales;
- any RFL practising from offices in England and Wales as an employee of a recognised sole practitioner; a manager, employee, owner or director of a recognised body; or as a manager, member or owner of a body corporate which is a manager, member or owner of a recognised body;

- in relation to 3.07–3.15 (acting for seller and buyer in conveyancing, property selling and mortgage related matters) and 3.16–3.22 (acting for lender and borrower in conveyancing transactions) only, an associated firm (see the definition in rule 24).

Rule 3 applies to overseas practice (15.03) except for 3.07–3.22 (acting for seller and buyer in conveyancing, property selling and mortgage related matters) if the land in question is situated outside England and Wales.

Rule 3 does not apply to solicitors, RELs or RFLs practising through or employed by a non-SRA authorised firm.

DUTY NOT TO ACT (3.01)

Rule 3.01 contains the basic prohibition not to act if there is a conflict of interests. The Code defines conflict as arising where (3.01(2)):

(a) you owe, or your firm owes, separate duties to act in the best interests of two or more clients in relation to the same or related matters, and those duties conflict, or there is a significant risk that those duties may conflict; or

(b) your duty to act in the best interests of any client in relation to a matter conflicts, or there is a significant risk that it may conflict, with your own interests in relation to that or a related matter.

Rule 3.01(3) states that a related matter will always include any other matter which involves the same asset or liability. Guidance notes 1–4 expand upon this interpretation of the term including the meaning of 'related matters'.

Further guidance was issued by the Law Society in June 2006 on the practical application of the Solicitors' Practice Rules (SPR) 1990, rule 16D and E (the former conflict and confidentiality and disclosure rules). Since the wording of 3.01 is virtually identical to the former practice rules, the guidance is equally relevant to 3.01. The guidance provides questions and answers on the former practice rules and gives practical examples and is reproduced in Appendix 1.

Notes 39–54 provide guidance on the prohibition in 3.01(2)(b), which states that a conflict exists where your duty to act in the best interests of a client in relation to a matter conflicts with (or there is a significant risk that it may conflict with) your own interests in relation to that matter. The notes confirm that there is no exception to this part of the rule – the exceptions in 3.02 (see below) have no application in relation to this part of the rule. The notes provide a non-exhaustive list of examples where this rule might apply. For example:

- where you buy from or sell to, lend to or borrow from your client;
- where you acquire publication rights with respect to the client's matter;
- where you become involved in a sexual relationship with the client;
- where you hold a power of attorney for a client;
- where you discover an act or omission that would justify a claim against you.

EXCEPTIONS TO DUTY NOT TO ACT (3.02)

There are two exceptions to the basic prohibition contained in rule 3.01. The first can be found in 3.02(1), the second in 3.02(2). Both exceptions require the clients affected to give their informed consent, in writing, to the firm acting despite the existence of a conflict.

Rule 3.02(1) contains the 'common interest' exception, allowing you or the firm to act if the different clients have a substantially common interest in relation to that matter or to a particular aspect of it. Note 6(a) provides detailed guidance on this exception. Further, the additional guidance (see Appendix 1), in paragraph 12, gives examples of the application of the 'common interest' exception. The second example (two partners, where one is buying out the interest of the other) makes it clear that in determining the 'common interest' it is not sufficient simply to look at the outcome of the matter. By itself, the common interest in completing the deal will not allow the firm to act if there is a conflict.

Rule 3.02(2) contains the exception allowing firms to act where there is a conflict and the clients are competing for the same asset which, if attained by one client, will make the asset unattainable to the other. Note 6(b) to rule 3 indicates that this exception is intended to apply to specialised areas of legal services where the clients are sophisticated users of those services and conclude that rather than seek out new advisers they would rather use their usual advisers in the knowledge that those advisers might also act for competing interests.

Examples of situations where this 'competing for the same asset exception' might apply can be found in note 6(b)(i); further guidance can be found in the additional guidance issued by the Law Society at paragraph 17 (see Appendix 1).

Where firms are legitimately acting for two or more clients, using the exception in 3.02(2), it is inevitable that the firm will possess confidential information concerning each client which might reasonably be regarded as relevant to the other client(s). As a result, where firms intend using this exception, the confidentiality rule (rule 4) must be considered. In particular consider the need for an information barrier to safeguard the clients' confidential information (for details, see Chapter 4).

In considering the application of these two exceptions, practitioners should carefully note the wording. Rule 3.02(1) commences with the words 'You or your firm may act ...'. Rule 3.02(2) commences with the words 'Your firm may act ...'. Where firms use 3.02(1) (common interest) it may be possible for an individual or a team to act for all parties, despite the conflict. Where firms use 3.02(2) (competing for the same asset) it would generally be necessary for different fee earners or teams to act for the different clients. This is confirmed in 3.02(2)(d) which states 'unless the clients specifically agree, no individual acts for, or is responsible for the supervision of, more than one of those clients'.

A test of reasonableness must be satisfied before reliance can be placed upon either of the exceptions in 3.02 (3.02(3)). Guidance notes 7 and 8 provide further information regarding this test.

Additional conditions for both the exceptions are contained in 3.02(4) as follows:

If you are relying on the exceptions in 3.02(1) or (2), you must:

(a) draw all the relevant issues to the attention of the clients before agreeing to act or, where already acting, when the conflict arises or as soon as is reasonably practicable, and in such a way that the clients concerned can understand the issues and the risks involved;

(b) have a reasonable belief that the clients understand the relevant issues; and

(c) be reasonably satisfied that those clients are of full capacity.

Guidance on 3.02(4) is to be found in note 9. Note 9(b) makes it clear that when a firm relies upon the 'common interest' exception, the need for informed consent requires you to identify by name the other client(s) or be able to do so when their identities are known. This coupled with compliance with 3.02(4) will satisfy the need for 'informed' consent. However, when relying upon the 'competing for the same asset' exception, it is not necessary to identify by name the other client(s) – compliance with 3.02(4) will satisfy the need for 'informed' consent.

CONFLICT WHEN ALREADY ACTING (3.03)

Rule 3.03 states that if a conflict arises between the interests of clients on a matter where you act or the firm acts for more than one of those clients, you or the firm may only continue to act for one of those clients provided the provisions of rule 4 (Confidentiality and disclosure) are complied with (see below, Chapter 4).

ACCEPTING GIFTS FROM CLIENTS (3.04)

Rule 3.04 applies where a client proposes to make a lifetime gift or a gift on death to or for the benefit of:

- you;
- any manager, owner or employee of the firm; or
- a family member of any of the above;

and the gift is of a significant amount.

The provisions do not prevent you (or other members of your firm or family members) receiving gifts from clients but do require the client to be advised to take independent advice about the gift if it is of a significant amount. 'Significant' for these purposes is defined either by the size of the gift itself or by having regard to the size of the client's estate and the reasonable expectations of the prospective beneficiaries. There is an obligation to stop acting if the client refuses to take this advice.

The 2009 Amendment Rules make it clear that the rule applies to proposed gifts to 'managers' of the firm.

The guidance notes cover the preparation of wills for family members (notes 56 and 57) and the interpretation of the definition of a 'significant amount' (notes 58–60).

PUBLIC OFFICE OR APPOINTMENT LEADING TO CONFLICT (3.05)

Rule 3.05 requires you to decline to act where you hold or a member of your firm or a manager, owner or employee of your firm holds a public office resulting in a conflict (or significant risk of a conflict). The requirement also applies even if there is no conflict or significant risk but where the public might conclude that the office might be used for the advantage of your client or where the appointment inhibits your ability to advise the client properly.

Note 63 gives examples of the public offices and appointments covered by 3.05.

ALTERNATIVE DISPUTE RESOLUTION (ADR) (3.06)

In relation to ADR, 3.06 sets out certain restrictions where you provide ADR services. In particular you must not:

(a) advise or act for any party in respect of a dispute in which you or any person within your firm is acting, or has acted, as mediator;

(b) provide ADR services in connection with a matter in which you or any person within your firm has acted for any party; or

(c) provide ADR services where you or any person within your firm has acted for any of the parties in issues not relating to the mediation, unless that has been disclosed to the parties and they consent to your acting.

The guidance (note 69) states that the SRA recommends that those offering ADR services should comply with a code of practice such as the Law Society's Code of Practice for Civil and Commercial Mediation and Code of Practice for Family Mediation. The current codes (both dated April 1999) can still be found in the archived 'Guide Online', at Annex 22A and Annex 22B (see **http://www.lawsociety.org.uk/professional/conduct/guideonline.law**).

CONVEYANCING, PROPERTY SELLING AND MORTGAGE RELATED SERVICES (3.07–3.22)

The provisions of 3.07–3.22 deal with conveyancing, property selling and mortgage related services. Rule 3.07 confirms that this section of rule 3 applies to both commercial and residential conveyancing and that the terms 'seller' and 'buyer' include a lessor and a lessee. The following points should be noted.

Conveyancing transactions at arm's length

Rule 3.08 states that you may act for seller and buyer when the transaction between the parties is not at arm's length and there is no conflict of interest. Note that this positive statement is subject to the prohibition in 10.06 (Dealing with more than one prospective buyer in a conveyancing transaction). Note 72 gives examples of transactions not usually regarded as being at arm's length.

Rule 3.09 sets out three exceptions where you may act for the seller and buyer subject to the conditions in 3.10. The three exceptions are:

- both parties are established clients;
- consideration is less than £10,000 and the transaction is not the grant of a lease; and
- the seller and buyer are represented by two separate offices in different localities.

The conditions set out in 3.10 are as follows:

(a) the written consent of both parties must be obtained;
(b) no conflict of interests must exist or arise;
(c) the seller must not be selling or leasing as a builder or developer; and
(d) when the seller and buyer are represented by two separate offices in different localities:

    (i) different individuals authorised to do the work, who normally work at each office, conduct or supervise the transaction for seller and buyer; and

    (ii) no office of the firm (or an associated firm) referred either client to the office conducting the transactions.

The 2009 Amendment Rules have replaced the original words with the words 'authorised to do the work' in (d)(i) above, acknowledging that firms may now employ or have as managers non-solicitors who are authorised to undertake conveyancing. Licensed conveyancers and RELs qualified to do conveyancing under regulation 12 of the European Communities (Lawyer's Practice) Regulations 2000 are examples of such persons.

Guidance on the exceptions contained in rule 3.09 can be found in notes 74–77.

Property selling and mortgage related services

Rule 3.11 allows you to act for seller and buyer where either the only way you are acting for the buyer is in providing mortgage related services or the only way you are acting for the seller is in providing property selling services through a Solicitors' Estate Agency Limited (SEAL).

The definition of a SEAL is contained in 3.12. This definition has been amended by the 2009 Amendment Rules. Previously the Code required a SEAL to be a recognised body. By definition, recognised bodies were incorporated bodies. Now, however, all firms (whether incorporated or not) must be recognised bodies or recognised sole practitioners. Consequently, the definition of a SEAL in the amended 3.12 requires the SEAL to be a recognised body which is a company. The definition requires the SEAL to be owned jointly by at least four participating firms which are not associated firms. 'Associated firms' means (rule 24) that the firms have one or more partners, members or owners in common. The definition of 'participating firm' has been amended by the 2009 Amendment Rules. Such firms are:

- recognised sole practitioners;
- recognised bodies; or
- authorised non-SRA firms;

where the firm itself is a manager or owner of the SEAL or where one or more of the firm's managers or owners is a manager or owner of the SEAL.

Consequently, as a result of this amendment one or more of the participating firms in a SEAL may be, for example, a firm of licensed conveyancers (authorised by the Council for Licensed Conveyancers – i.e. a non-SRA firm).

Finally, no participating firm in a SEAL can have majority control of the SEAL and the SEAL must be conducted from accommodation physically divided from, and clearly differentiated from, that of any participating firm.

The conditions for acting under 3.11 are set out in 3.13 and apply where you are acting for buyer and seller and either you are acting for the buyer in providing mortgage related services or you are acting through a SEAL for the seller.

Conflict arising when acting for seller and buyer

Rule 3.15 confirms that if conflict arises during the course of a transaction in which you are acting for both parties, you can continue to act for one party providing the conditions in rule 4 (Confidentiality and disclosure) are satisfied.

Acting for the lender and borrower in conveyancing transactions

The provisions of 3.16–3.22 apply to acting for lender and borrower in conveyancing transactions. They apply to both commercial and residential conveyancing transactions and the term 'mortgage' includes a remortgage.

The basic prohibition against acting for lender and borrower on the grant of a mortgage of land appears in 3.16(2). In no circumstances can you act for both parties if a conflict of interests exists or arises. Otherwise the ability to act for both the lender and borrower depends on whether the mortgage is an individual mortgage at arm's length (where acting for both parties is prohibited) or a standard mortgage (where acting for both parties is permitted subject to conditions). Rule 3.17 defines the terms 'standard mortgage' and 'individual mortgage'.

Rule 3.18 imposes an obligation to notify the lender of certain circumstances where the solicitor wishes to act for lender and borrower on the grant of a standard mortgage. The notifiable circumstances are where you propose to act for the seller, buyer and lender in the same transaction or where the prospective borrower is:

(i) the firm or any of its managers or owners, or a member of their immediate family;
(ii) an associated firm, any of its managers or owners, or a member of their immediate family; and/or
(iii) the individual conducting or supervising the transaction, or a member of their immediate family …

The 2009 Amendment Rules have extended the requirement to notify to include the circumstances where the firm is the prospective borrower. Note also that the notification requirements arise where the borrower is a manager or owner of a firm (i.e. to include a non-solicitor lawyer or a non-lawyer) or where the individual conducting and supervising the transaction is the borrower (again including a non-solicitor lawyer).

Where it is possible for a firm to act for both the lender and borrower on a standard mortgage, the lender's instructions must not extend beyond certain limitations set out in 3.19 and 3.21. Further in residential loans, the instructions must permit the use of the certificate of title required by 3.20. Notes 81–88 provide further guidance on the obligations applicable when acting for lender and borrower in conveyancing transactions.

GUIDANCE ON CONFLICT

In addition to the specific guidance notes mentioned above, there are comprehensive guidance notes on the following:

- Limited/defined retainers (notes 12 and 13). These notes explain that it might be possible to act for two or more clients by limiting the retainer so as to define the areas of conflict you cannot advise upon.
- Professional embarrassment (notes 14–16). These notes point out that there may be circumstances when you should refuse to act even though there is no conflict of interests but nonetheless you feel unable to act in the best interests of a client because of some form of professional embarrassment. Note 15 extends the guidance on embarrassment to situations where, through the use of an information barrier and in accordance with the confidentiality and disclosure rules (rule 4) the firm can act for a client even though it has information relevant to that client that cannot be disclosed because of the duty of confidentiality owed to another client.
- In-house practice (notes 17–22). These notes identify the circumstances when conflict can arise in-house, i.e. where an in-house lawyer is employed, thus making the employer the client.

- Co-defendants (notes 23–35). These notes provide comprehensive guidance on the position when a solicitor is asked to advise co-defendants. In particular note 25 provides examples of where conflict might arise in these circumstances. There is also limited guidance on the regulations in publicly funded cases (see notes 23 and 33).
- Mediation (note 36). This note confirms that there is no objection to you acting as a conciliator and mediator between parties.
- Local authority client (note 37). This note highlights the risk of tendering for local authority work where such work is likely to give rise to conflicts between existing clients and the local authority.
- Insolvency practice (note 38). Licensed insolvency practitioners should consider relationships with clients that might affect their ability to accept an appointment to administer an insolvent estate or bankruptcy. (For insolvency practice generally, see rule 17 (below, Chapter 17).)

POSSIBLE FUTURE AMENDMENTS

The consultation paper noted above suggests amendments to rule 3 which would substantially extend the existing exceptions in rules 3.02(1) and (2) to allow firms to be able to act with the informed consent of two or more clients in any other situation, not involving litigation, where there is a conflict of interests. The change, if made, would be subject to tight controls and record keeping obligations. The reasons given for the suggested change include the fact that many legal jurisdictions (including European and US jurisdictions) allow lawyers to waive their conflict obligations by giving informed consent and the current UK law does not prevent such a waiver. It is likely that any change brought about would only apply to 'sophisticated clients'.

CONCLUSION

The 2009 Amendment Rules do not really make any significant changes to the obligations contained in rule 3. However, the scope of many of the obligations is extended to cover all employees and all managers (whether they are lawyers or not). The definition of a SEAL has changed, allowing for non-SRA authorised firms to participate in such a body and solicitors involved with SEALs should check that their current arrangements satisfy the new definition.

CHAPTER 4

Confidentiality and disclosure

INTRODUCTION

Rule 4 sets out the provisions relating to confidentiality and disclosure. The following topics are covered in rule 4:

- Duty of confidentiality
- Duty of disclosure
- Duty not to put confidentiality at risk by acting
- Exceptions to duty not to put confidentiality at risk by acting

At the time of writing, the SRA has issued a consultation paper on amendments to rule 4 (with responses required by 31 March 2009). Brief details of these proposed changes appear in this chapter.

SCOPE

Rule 4 applies (where the context provides) to:

- solicitors or RELs practising from offices in England and Wales (including recognised sole practitioners practising as solicitors or RELs);
- recognised bodies (all practices other than recognised sole practitioners must now be recognised bodies);
- any other person who is a manager or employee of a recognised body or the employee of a recognised sole practitioner practising from offices in England and Wales;
- any RFL practising from offices in England and Wales as an employee of a recognised sole practitioner; a manager, employee, owner or director of a recognised body; or as a manager, member or owner of a body corporate which is a manager, member or owner of a recognised body.

Rule 4 applies in full to overseas practice (15.04).

Rule 4 does not apply to solicitors, RELs or RFLs practising through or employed by a non-SRA authorised firm.

DUTY OF CONFIDENTIALITY (4.01)

The provisions of 4.01 require you and your firm to keep the affairs of clients and former clients confidential except where disclosure is required or permitted by law or by the client or former client. Notes 3–6 to rule 4 provide guidance on this basic duty confirming that the duty applies to information acquired from a prospective client (see note 6).

The notes also provide guidance on when you may have to disclose confidential information despite the basic rule. In insolvency situations there may be an obligation to disclose what might appear to be confidential information to a liquidator or trustee in bankruptcy (note 7). Other circumstances listed in the notes where disclosure might be required or permitted include:

- where a statute empowers the government and other bodies to seek information (e.g. HM Revenue and Customs) (note 9);
- where the reporting requirements in the Proceeds of Crime Act 2002 override the duty of confidentiality (note 10);
- if the requirements of the Freedom of Information Act 2000 apply (generally these requirements affect certain public bodies and therefore are only likely to apply to in-house lawyers) (note 11);
- if it is necessary to prevent a crime that you reasonably believe is likely to result in serious bodily harm (note 12);
- circumstances involving children (notes 13 and 14); and
- where the court orders (note 15). See also notes 16–19 for further examples.

DUTY OF DISCLOSURE (4.02)

Rule 4.02 requires disclosure to a client of all information of which you are aware which is material to that client's matter regardless of the source of that information. The obligation is restricted to lawyers or other fee earners and applies where you are personally acting on a matter, whether individually or as one of a group, or on a matter you are personally supervising. Note 20 confirms that the duty is restricted to information of which you are aware and does not extend to information of which others in the firm may be aware. However, passing the client on to another fee earner who is not aware of the information should only be considered a possible solution if the client agrees to this – see note 23. Note 24 gives guidance on the meaning of 'information which is material to that client's matter'.

As well as being a fundamental principle, the duty of disclosure is highly relevant when deciding whether or not a firm can act against a former client. Previously a conflict of interests could arise in such circumstances, thus preventing the firm from acting against a former client. The firm would owe a duty of confidentiality to the former client but if the information held by the firm was material to the new client, it had to be disclosed. This led to a conflict between the duties owed to the former client and those owed to the new client.

Rule 4.02 resolves the position by providing that the duty to disclose is always subject to the duty in confidentiality, which always overrides the duty to disclose. However, note 22 to rule 4 states that the failure to disclose relevant information cannot be excused simply because that disclosure would breach a separate duty of confidentiality. Consideration should be given to varying the terms of the retainer between the solicitor and client so that the inability to disclose is not a breach of the duty owed to the client. Including a clause to this effect in the firm's terms of business might be one way to achieve this. However, this approach does not mean that it is proper in all circumstances to act against a former client. Rule 4.03 (Duty not to put confidentiality at risk by acting – see below) must also be considered in these cases. Acting against former (or current) clients should now be treated as a confidentiality issue rather than a conflict issue.

The duty of disclosure does not apply (4.02(b)):

(i)   where such disclosure is prohibited by law;
(ii) where it is agreed expressly that no duty to disclose arises or a different standard of disclosure applies; or
(iii) where you reasonably believe that serious physical or mental injury will be caused to any person if the information is disclosed to a client.

Note 20 provides instances where the disclosure is prohibited by law. These include:

- where the money laundering legislation prohibits the disclosure (e.g. the tipping off offence in the Proceeds of Crime Act 2002, s.333A);
- where it is obvious that privileged documents have been mistakenly disclosed;
- where the solicitor comes into possession of information relating to state security or intelligence matters to which the Official Secrets Act 1989 applies.

DUTY NOT TO PUT CONFIDENTIALITY AT RISK BY ACTING (4.03)

Rule 4.03 states that if you hold or your firm holds confidential information relating to a client or former client, you must not risk breaching confidentiality by acting or continuing to act for another client if two conditions apply:

- the information might reasonably be expected to be material; and
- the client has an interest adverse to the first-mentioned client or former client.

Exceptions to 4.03 can be found in 4.04 and 4.05 (see below).

Unlike the duty of disclosure which applies to information held by an individual and not to information held by other members of the firm (see note 20), the duty not to act in 4.03 applies whether the confidential information is held by you or by your firm.

Both conditions in 4.03 must apply before the restriction on acting applies. Notes 27 and 28 provide guidance on the meaning of 'adverse interest'. Further illustrations and examples can be found in the additional guidance on SPR 1990, rule 16E issued by the Law Society and reproduced in Appendix 1.

EXCEPTION TO DUTY NOT TO PUT CONFIDENTIALITY AT RISK BY ACTING – WITH CLIENTS' CONSENT (4.04)

A firm may act or continue to act for a client despite the restriction in 4.03 if both clients give their informed consent (4.04(1)). The definition of 'both clients' in this context can be found in 4.04(2).

Note 34 provides guidance on 'informed consent'. It confirms that the identity of each client and the nature of the client's business are confidential and in consequence there may be occasions where it is impossible to seek consent without breaching the duty of confidentiality owed to the other client. The note does, however, suggest that there may be circumstances where sufficient information can be given in order to obtain 'informed consent' even if the identity of the other client(s) and the nature of their particular interest(s) are not disclosed.

Sophisticated clients can provide their consent for these purposes at the beginning of a retainer through standard terms of business (see note 35). Reliance upon such a clause would be subject to the requirement of reasonableness (see below).

Rule 4.04(1) contains four further conditions:

(a) the client for whom you act or are proposing to act knows that your firm, or a lawyer or other fee earner of your firm, holds, or might hold, material information (in circumstances described in 4.03) in relation to their matter which you cannot disclose;

It is important when relying upon the exception in 4.04 to ensure that the client for whom the firm is acting is aware that material information cannot be disclosed and that they consent to this fact as part of their 'informed consent'. There is no reason why such agreement should not be contained in the firm's standard terms of business; however, it should be brought specifically to the client's attention in order to satisfy the requirement for 'informed consent'.

(b) you have a reasonable belief that both clients understand the relevant issues after these have been brought to their attention;

Each case will be different and the reference to 'reasonable' belief suggests an objective test will be applied in the event of a complaint. The relevant issues must include the risks involved and, where the firm is currently acting for both clients, the possibility that if a conflict arises it may have to cease to act for one or both clients. Note 34 states: '... generally it will be only sophisticated clients, for example, a corporate body with in-house legal advisers or other appropriate expertise, who will have the expertise and ability to weigh up the issues and the risks of giving consent on the basis of the information they have been given'.

   (c) both clients have agreed to the conditions under which you will be acting or continuing to act; ...

The condition in (c) refers to the information barrier which should be erected in order to preserve the client's (or former client's) confidential information. Where reliance is placed upon the exception in 4.03, the clients' agreement can extend to the nature of the arrangements for the information barrier. This provides the firm with a degree of flexibility when erecting the barrier (see note 33). The necessary safeguards for information barriers are set out in detail in notes 41–45. In particular the arrangements outlined in note 44(a)–(f) would normally be appropriate to demonstrate the adequacy of an information barrier when acting in accordance with 4.04.

   (d) it is reasonable in all the circumstances to do so.

Reliance upon the exception in 4.04 is dependent upon reasonableness. Again, this suggests that an objective test will be used if a complaint is received.

EXCEPTION TO DUTY NOT TO PUT CONFIDENTIALITY AT RISK BY ACTING – WITHOUT CLIENTS' CONSENT (4.05)

You may to continue to act on an existing matter or on a matter related to an existing matter in the circumstances prohibited by 4.03 without the consent of the client for whom confidential information is held (or might be held).

   This provision has potential application where it might not be possible to obtain the consent of both clients (e.g. it may be impossible to approach the client for consent without breaching the duty of confidentiality owed to the other client – see above) or where an approach has been made but the client refuses to give consent.

   However, there is a major point of contrast between the exceptions in 4.04 (consent) and 4.05 (non-consent). Rule 4.04 permits a firm to act or continue to act if the conditions of the rule apply; 4.05 only permits a firm to continue to act on an existing matter or on a matter related to an existing matter. The only way that a firm can take on a new matter in circumstances where the restriction in 4.03 applies is with both clients' consent (see note 37).

   One situation where 4.05 (non-consent) might be appropriate is where two or more firms amalgamate – see note 39.

   As with 4.04, 4.05 contains a further four conditions:

   (a) it is not possible to obtain informed consent under 4.04 above from the client for whom your firm, or a lawyer or other fee earner of your firm, holds, or might hold, material confidential information;

This condition suggests that it is necessary for informed consent to be obtained where this is possible. It would not be appropriate to rely upon 4.05

without considering whether an approach to the client to obtain their consent is possible. The exception should only be applied if, after due consideration, the firm decides that an approach to the client is impossible or an approach has been made but the client refuses consent.

> (b) your client has agreed to your acting in the knowledge that your firm, or a lawyer or other fee earner of your firm, holds, or might hold, information material to their matter which you cannot disclose;

This condition is similar to the condition in 4.04 (see above). Again this might be resolved by including an appropriate clause in the firm's standard terms of business.

> (c) any safeguards which comply with the standards required by law at the time they are implemented are put in place; ...

This condition must be distinguished from the equivalent condition in 4.04. It refers to the information barrier but where the client whose confidential information is being protected does not consent to the firm acting, a higher standard of safeguards must be implemented (see note 36). The leading case on information barriers and the standards required by law is the House of Lords decision in *Prince Jefri Bolkiah* v. *KPMG* [1999] 2 WLR 215. Notes 41–45 are again relevant with note 44 setting out additional arrangements (note 44(g)–(n)) which may be appropriate when acting under 4.05.

> (d) it is reasonable in all the circumstances to do so.

The same comments noted above will be relevant in respect of this condition.

POSSIBLE FUTURE AMENDMENTS

The consultation paper noted above suggests amendments to rule 4 which would allow a firm holding confidential information for one client to accept instructions from a new client where there is adversity between the clients without the first client's consent. At present, the rule only allows this where the firm has already started acting for the new client before the problem arises. The proposal would extend this to allow a firm to take on instructions in this situation provided an information barrier which complies with the requirements of the common law can be put in place.

The arguments in favour of these changes are:

- if a common law compliant information barrier is put in place, confidential information is protected to the very high standards required by the law and further protection is unnecessary;
- the need to seek consent may increasingly lead to clients instructing firms tactically to deny their competitors access to the best specialist advice;
- the rule prevents law firms in this country acting in situations where other professional advisers and overseas law firms are able to do so.

31

CONCLUSION

The 2009 Amendment Rules do not really make any significant changes to the obligations contained in rule 4. However, the scope of many of the obligations is extended to cover all employees and all managers (whether they are lawyers or not). The following checklist identifies some matters to consider.

Duty to disclose

Fee earners must be made aware of the requirements to disclose to a client all information that is material to that client's matter. They should appreciate that this duty only applies to information known to the individual and does not extend to information of which others in the firm may be aware. While the duty is always subject to confidentiality, the firm's procedures should be reviewed to take into account the following:

- the possibility of another fee earner in the firm taking on the work;
- obtaining the consent of the client to the fact that material information may be known but cannot be disclosed or used (the firm's terms of business may be amended);
- authorisation within the firm – who should authorise another fee earner to take on such a matter when there is information held within the firm relevant but confidential?
- the test of 'reasonableness' should always be applied.

Duty not to put confidentiality at risk by acting

Principals must ensure that fee earners are aware of this duty. They must decide whether to take advantage of the permitted exceptions and, if so, who should authorise the use of the exceptions.

Where the exceptions are applied, creation of appropriate information barriers will be necessary. Systems must be put in place (depending upon whether clients have consented or not) by reference to the detailed guidance in notes 41–45.

Acting against former clients

The issues involved in acting against former clients are relevant to many firms. The managers of firms should ensure that fee earners are made aware of the appropriate procedures that must be followed in determining whether it is possible to act against former clients. The firm's system might require fee earners to consider the following questions when deciding to act for a client (A) against a former client (B):

- Does the firm hold confidential information in relation to B which might reasonably be expected to be material to A? If not, subject to the question of 'embarrassment', the firm should not be prohibited from acting simply because of the former client relationship with B.
- If the firm does hold confidential information in relation to B which might reasonably be expected to be material to A, the person holding such information cannot act for A since to do so would put the confidential information at risk – confidentiality can be breached by giving advice which is tainted by the confidential information. If there is no adverse interest between A and B it might, subject to rule 4, be possible for another fee earner in the firm to act for A.
- Does A have an interest adverse to B? If this is the case rule 4.03 will prevent the firm from acting for A, even if it is proposed that someone other than the fee earner who acted for B should act, unless an exception applies.
- If rule 4.03 applies, does an exception nevertheless allow the firm to act? If 4.03 does apply and both A and B give their informed consent then, subject to the other conditions, 4.04 will allow the firm to act or continue to act for A. If B does not consent (or it is impossible to seek B's consent) then, subject to the conditions, 4.05 may allow the firm to continue to act on an existing matter or on a matter related to an existing matter.

CHAPTER 5

Business management in England and Wales

INTRODUCTION

Rule 5 deals with the supervision and management of a solicitor's firm or in-house practice. It only applies to practice in England and Wales (overseas offices are covered by rule 15 – see below). It imposes extensive obligations relating to business management. The introduction to the rule states that the terms 'supervision' and 'management' refer to:

- the professional overseeing of staff and client matters;
- the overall direction and development of the practice;
- the day-to-day administration of the practice.

Many firms will have adopted management systems that will satisfy the requirements of rule 5. However, since the rule makes such systems mandatory, it will be necessary for firms to review their systems, make such changes as necessary and ensure that, if called upon, adequate evidence is available to demonstrate compliance.

The following topics are covered by the rule:

- Supervision and management responsibilities
- Persons who must be 'qualified to supervise'
- Supervision of work for clients and members of the public

SCOPE

- Rule 5.01(1) (supervision and management responsibilities) applies to a recognised body, a manager of a recognised body, or a recognised sole practitioner.
- Rule 5.01(2) (in-house management responsibilities) applies to a solicitor or an REL employed as head of an in-house legal department.
- Rule 5.03 (supervision of work for clients and members of the public) applies to a recognised body, a manager of a recognised body, or a recognised sole practitioner. It also applies to an in-house solicitor or REL who is required to be 'qualified to supervise'.

Rule 5 does not apply to overseas practice but compliance with 15.05(2) to (4) is required as follows:

- restrictions on setting up as a solicitor sole practitioner or as an REL sole practitioner (15.05(2));
- obligations relating to non-recognised bodies controlled by solicitors and/ or RELs (15.05(3));
- proper management and supervision (15.05(4)).

Rule 5 does not apply to solicitors, RELs or RFLs practising through or employed by a non-SRA authorised firm.

SUPERVISION AND MANAGEMENT RESPONSIBILITIES (5.01)

Rule 5.01(1)(a) requires a recognised body, a manager of a recognised body, or a recognised sole practitioner to make arrangements for effective management of the firm as a whole and in particular provide for 'compliance by the firm and its managers with the duties of a principal, in law and conduct, to exercise appropriate supervision over all staff, and ensure proper supervision and direction of clients' matters'. Note 5 confirms that firms will be expected to produce evidence of a systematic and effective approach to management. The note suggests that this approach may include the implementation of one or more of (for example):

- the guidance issued by the SRA or the Law Society;
- the firm's own documented standards;
- the Lexcel standard or other practice management standards promoted by the Law Society;
- the guidelines for accounting procedures (see Appendix 3 to the Solicitors' Accounts Rules 1998);
- external quality standards; and/or
- in the case of in-house lawyers, standards laid down by their management or other appropriate body.

There is further guidance on the requirements of 5.01(1)(a) in notes 8–13.

Rule 5.01(1) contains a further 11 specific areas of management which must be addressed as part of a principal's supervision and management responsibilities. These are as follows.

Compliance with the money laundering regulations (5.01(1)(b))

Where applicable, firms must have policies that ensure compliance with the regulations and in particular must adopt appropriate internal anti-money laundering systems (for details of such systems see, for example, Peter Camp, *Solicitors and Money Laundering: A Compliance Manual* (Law Society Publishing, 3rd edn, 2009)). Note 14 provides further limited guidance.

Compliance with key regulatory requirements (5.01(1)(c))

This covers systems for ensuring key regulatory requirements are met including those relating to:

- practising certificates;
- registration of RELs and RFLs;
- recognition of all forms of practice (i.e. a recognised sole practitioner or a recognised body – recognition by the SRA is now an annual requirement);
- indemnity insurance cover;
- delivery of accountants' reports;
- co-operation with and reporting obligations to the SRA.

The obligations in relation to these matters are all imposed elsewhere. However, the management arrangements must specifically include policies relating to how these obligations are dealt with internally. Notes 15–18 provide additional guidance on these matters.

Identification of conflicts of interests (5.01(1)(d))

The definition of a conflict is contained in rule 3 (see above, Chapter 3). Note 19 to rule 5 states that the firm should have a systematic approach to identifying and avoiding conflicts of interests, dealing with the conflicts between duties of confidentiality and disclosure, and maintaining client confidentiality (see above, Chapter 4). Some form of 'conflict search' procedure should be adopted for new clients but the system should also ensure that conflicts arising during the course of a retainer are identified and properly dealt with.

Compliance with rule 2 on client care, costs information and complaints handling (5.01(1)(e))

The requirements of rule 2 are dealt with in Chapter 2 above. One way of complying with these requirements is to adopt a firm-wide policy by designing engagement letters and/or terms of business to be used for all clients, rather than leaving it to the individual fee earner to determine the information given to clients at the outset of a retainer. Further limited guidance is contained in note 20.

Control of undertakings (5.01(1)(f))

Obligations arising from undertakings are dealt with in rule 10 (see below, Chapter 10). Management should be aware of the firm's outstanding liabilities and should impose limitations on who can give undertakings on behalf of the firm.

Safekeeping of documents and assets entrusted to the firm (5.01(1)(g))

Notes 22–23 provide guidance on this topic. 'Assets' include client money, wills, deeds, investments and other property entrusted to the firm by clients and others. The minimum requirement is the ability to identify to whom the documents and assets belong and in connection with which matter. Inevitably, this means that records of such assets should be maintained. The Solicitors' Financial Services (Conduct of Business) Rules 2001 require a record of documents of title to certain investments kept by the firm. Rule 5.01(1)(g) effectively extends the requirement to all other assets entrusted to the firm.

Compliance with equality and diversity rule (5.01(1)(h))

For guidance on complying with rule 6 (Equality and diversity) see below, Chapter 6.

Training (5.01(1)(i))

Management systems must address the issue of training individuals in the firm so as to achieve a level of competence appropriate to their work and level of responsibility. Training needs should not be left to the individual but must be dealt with systematically by the firm's principals. The 2009 Amendment Rules have extended many obligations in the Code to non-solicitor lawyers and non-lawyer managers and employees. Training should be provided on relevant parts of the Code and other regulations (e.g. the Solicitors' Accounts Rules 1998). See the SRA's guidance, 'New duties for employees and firms' at **www.sra.org.uk/code-of-conduct/guidance/2405.article**. Notes 25–30 provide additional guidance on training.

Financial control (5.01(1)(j))

Principals must exercise adequate oversight of the firm's own financial arrangements (see note 31). Consequently, the requirement to address financial control in the overall management framework is mandatory. There is no prescribed system but firms should look forward rather than just relying upon historic records. Day-to-day financial control may be delegated to suitable staff.

Practice continuity (5.01(1)(k))

Management systems must ensure that there is proper continuation of the practice in the event of absences due to emergencies, with minimum interruption to clients' business. Business continuity policies must form part of a firm's overall management framework.

The notes provide additional guidance on this area (see notes 32–38). While there is some general guidance relevant to all types of practice, the majority of the notes concentrate on systems that are necessary for sole practitioners to adopt. In particular, sole practitioners should consider:

- making adequate provision for the running of the practice in the event of death or permanent disability by a person who is 'qualified to supervise' (note 32);
- making adequate arrangements in advance to meet unforeseen circumstances in relation to the conduct of clients' affairs and the administration of the practice. Arrangements should be with another solicitor (or REL) to supervise the firm until the sole practitioner returns. The firm's bankers should be notified in advance, allowing the solicitor (or REL) covering the absence to operate client and office accounts (note 35);
- obtaining the permission of the SRA for another solicitor to complete a sole practitioner's application for a practising certificate when the absence lasts beyond the period covered by the practising certificate (note 36).

The notes also cover the position of a sole practitioner who is struck off or suspended (note 37) or who wishes to stop practising (note 38).

Management of risk (5.01(1)(l))

The firm's management policies must include arrangements for risk assessment, including a requirement for periodic reviews of the firm's risk profile (see note 39).

Note 40 provides that, ideally, risk assessment should not be limited to professional negligence but should also cover:

- complaints (including a complaints log);
- client related credit risks and exposure;
- claims under legislation (e.g. data protection);
- IT failures and abuses;
- damage to offices.

In-house practice (5.01(2))

Rule 5.01(2) applies to a solicitor or an REL employed as the head of an in-house legal department. The supervision and management requirements applicable in these circumstances must provide for:

(a) adequate supervision and direction of those assisting in your in-house practice;
(b) control of undertakings; and
(c) identification of conflicts of interests.

Note 41 gives further, limited guidance. The topic of in-house practice is dealt with in more detail in rule 13 (see below, Chapter 13).

PERSONS WHO MUST BE 'QUALIFIED TO SUPERVISE' (5.02)

Rule 5.02 sets out the requirements applicable to who is 'qualified to supervise' and in what circumstances must an office of a firm have in attendance such a person. Prior to 1 July 2007 it was necessary for each office of a firm to have at least one solicitor so qualified in full-time attendance. The requirement is now that the following persons must be 'qualified to supervise' (5.02(1)):

(a) a recognised sole practitioner;
(b) one of the lawyer managers of a recognised body or of a body corporate which is a manager of the recognised body;
(c) one of the solicitors or RELs employed by a law centre; or
(d) one in-house solicitor or in-house REL in any department where solicitors and/ or RELs, as part of that employment:

    (i) do publicly funded work; or
    (ii) do or supervise advocacy or the conduct of proceedings for members of the public before a court or immigration tribunal.

This requirement has been amended as a result of the 2009 Amendment Rules. Generally the amendment brings the wording in line with the new structures introduced in the Legal Services Act 2007. However, it should be noted that any recognised sole practitioner must be 'qualified to supervise'. In respect of any other recognised body (i.e. a partnership, LLP or company) there must be at least one lawyer manager who is 'qualified to supervise'. This could mean someone who is a lawyer albeit not a solicitor. Where a recognised body has individual managers who are not lawyers, these individuals will not be 'qualified to supervise'.

Note 42 makes it clear that the responsibilities imposed on the person 'qualified to supervise' relate to management of the firm rather than supervision of particular work. Being 'qualified to supervise' does not give the right to non-solicitor lawyer managers to undertake all forms of reserved legal activities. The scope of reserved legal activities which can be undertaken by non-solicitor lawyers is dealt with in rule 12 (see Chapter 12).

The definition of 'qualified to supervise' appears in 5.02(2). To be so qualified, a person must:

(a) have completed the training specified from time to time by the SRA for this purpose; and
(b) have been entitled to practise as a lawyer for at least 36 months within the last 10 years;

and be able to demonstrate this if asked by the SRA.

Note 44 expands on the training specified by the SRA. This is attendance at or participation in any course(s) or programme(s) of learning on management skills for a minimum of 12 hours. The courses do not have to attract accreditation under the continuing professional development (CPD) scheme. This is a fairly flexible definition. Management courses on any of the areas mentioned in 5.01(1)(a)–(l) should be capable of falling within this definition. In addition to general management training, other examples might include courses on:

- management of anti-money laundering procedures;
- financial control;
- risk management;
- equality and diversity.

The term 'qualified to supervise' appeared in SPR 1990, rule 13 where the definition was the same. SPR 1990, rule 13 came into effect on 23 December 1999. Any management courses taken before or after that date will count towards the necessary 12 hours' management training. Those who are 'qualified to supervise' should have access to an appropriate training record to demonstrate their attendance if asked to do so by the SRA.

Rule 5.02(2)(b) requires the person 'qualified to supervise' to have been entitled to practise as a lawyer for at least 36 months within the last 10 years. This means that, as noted above, the person so qualified does not have to be a solicitor. A lawyer is defined in rule 24 for these purposes as:

> a member of one of the following professions, entitled to practise as such:
>
> (a) the profession of solicitor, barrister or advocate of the UK;
> (b) a profession whose members are authorised to practise by an approved regulator other than the Solicitors Regulation Authority;
> (c) an Establishment Directive profession other than a UK profession;
> (d) a legal profession which has been approved by the Solicitors Regulation Authority for the purpose of recognised bodies in England and Wales; or
> (e) any other regulated legal profession which is recognised as such by the Solicitors Regulation Authority; ...

The 'approved regulators' (other than the SRA) listed in the Legal Services Act 2007, Sched.4 are:

- the General Council of the Bar (regulating barristers);
- the Master of the Faculties (regulating notaries);
- the Institute of Legal Executives (regulating legal executives);
- the Council for Licensed Conveyancers (regulating licensed conveyancers);
- the Chartered Institute of Patent Attorneys (regulating patent agents);
- the Institute of Trade Mark Attorneys (regulating trade mark attorneys);
- the Association of Law Costs Draftsmen (regulating law costs draftsmen).

For solicitors, holding a practising certificate for a period of 36 months in the past 10 years would normally be sufficient evidence of compliance with this requirement. For other lawyers it will be necessary to show that the individual has been entitled to practise as such a lawyer for at least 36 months in the past 10 years.

Note 33 states that if you are away from the office for a month or more and you are the only person 'qualified to supervise', arrangements made for business continuity (see above) would normally have to include the provision for another person 'qualified to supervise' to attend your office.

SUPERVISION OF WORK FOR CLIENTS AND MEMBERS OF THE PUBLIC (5.03)

The provisions in 5.01 and 5.02 concentrate on management issues (as noted above, the responsibilities imposed on the person 'qualified to supervise' relate to management of the firm rather than supervision of particular work).

Client work supervision is dealt with in 5.03. It imposes specific standards relating to the supervision of client matters.

Rule 5.03(1) provides a general statement requiring a recognised body, a manager of a recognised body or a recognised sole practitioner to ensure that the firm has in place a system for supervising clients' matters. This must be undertaken by a suitably experienced and competent person but no particular qualification is called for (see note 46). Consequently the individual undertaking the supervision need not be a person 'qualified to supervise' as defined in 5.02.

In-house solicitors or RELs who are required to be 'qualified to supervise' must ensure a system is in place for supervising work undertaken for members of the public (5.03(2)).

As a result of 5.03(3), the system adopted for supervision must include appropriate and effective procedures under which the quality of work undertaken for clients and members of the public is checked with reasonable regularity by a suitably experienced and competent person. This effectively means that firms must introduce a form of file review for all fee earners (including the principals in the firm). The notes provide helpful guidance on this requirement. In particular:

- The supervisor should have sufficient legal knowledge and experience to identify problems with the quality of work but need not be an expert (note 47).
- The requirements of the rule apply to wherever members of staff work, including home or through a 'virtual' office (note 48).
- Supervision must be undertaken by someone who is genuinely part of the practice – it cannot be delegated to someone outside the control of the principals (note 49).
- If a complaint is made it will be necessary to demonstrate that the work-checking requirements are appropriate, effective and undertaken with reasonable regularity (note 50).

- The supervision in accordance with 5.03 embraces all aspects of clients' work including handling client money and compliance with rule 2 (Client relations) (note 52).

CONCLUSION

The 2009 Amendment Rules do not really make any significant changes to the obligations contained in rule 5. However, the scope of the obligations is extended to cover the recognised body, a manager of a recognised body and a recognised sole practitioner. Rule 5 contains some substantial obligations relating to business management procedures. The following checklist identifies the main requirements.

Management framework

- You must ensure that there is evidence of a systematic and effective approach to management in relation to at least the 12 heads contained in 5.01:
    - supervision and management responsibilities;
    - compliance with money laundering regulations;
    - compliance with key regulatory requirements;
    - identification of conflicts of interests;
    - compliance with rule 2 (client care, costs information and complaints);
    - control of undertakings;
    - safekeeping of documents and assets;
    - compliance with rule 6 (Equality and diversity);
    - training;
    - financial control;
    - practice continuity;
    - risk management.

- In relation to each of the above heads, the evidence indicating a systematic and effective approach may be by reference to an appropriate standard or guidance issued by the Law Society, SRA or an external provider. Where this is the case, the appropriate standard, etc. should be clearly documented.

Qualified to supervise

By reference to the practice, a check should be made to identify who must, within the practice, be 'qualified to supervise'. The person(s) who is/are 'qualified to supervise' should be identified in accordance with the rule. The list of persons who can now be 'qualified to supervise' has been extended by the new definition of those who are entitled to practise as a lawyer. However, non-solicitor lawyers (who may be qualified to supervise) are restricted in the types of reserved activities they can undertake in a firm. Evidence that the person(s) is/are so qualified should be properly recorded.

Supervision of client matters

The firm must adopt appropriate procedures to satisfy the requirements of 5.03, including the checking of the quality of work undertaken for clients and members of the public.

CHAPTER 6

Equality and diversity

INTRODUCTION

Rule 6 imposes obligations in relation to equality and diversity. The introduction to the rule makes it clear that the duties imposed by the rule are in addition to and not in substitution for obligations imposed by anti-discrimination legislation.

The following topics are covered by the rule:

- Duty not to discriminate
- Equality and diversity policy

SCOPE

Rule 6 applies to:

- solicitors or RELs practising from offices in England and Wales (including recognised sole practitioners practising as solicitors or RELs);
- recognised bodies (all practices other than recognised sole practitioners must now be recognised bodies);
- any other person who is a manager or employee of a recognised body or the employee of a recognised sole practitioner practising from offices in England and Wales;
- any RFL practising from offices in England and Wales as an employee of a recognised sole practitioner; a manager, employee, owner or director of a recognised body; or as a manager, member or owner of a body corporate which is a manager, member or owner of a recognised body.

Rule 6 does not apply to overseas practice but the core duties (rule 1) will always apply (see 15.06).

Rule 6 does not apply to solicitors, RELs or RFLs practising through or employed by a non-SRA authorised firm.

DUTY NOT TO DISCRIMINATE (6.01)

The duty not to discriminate is set out in 6.01. Rule 6.01(1) provides:

> You must not in your professional dealings with the firm's managers and employees, other lawyers, clients or third parties discriminate, without lawful cause, against any person, nor victimise or harass them on the grounds of:
>
> (a) race or racial group (including colour, nationality and ethnic or national origins);
> (b) sex (including marital status, gender reassignment, pregnancy, maternity and paternity);
> (c) sexual orientation (including civil partnership status);
> (d) religion or belief;
> (e) age; or
> (f) disability.

Note that 'gender assignment, pregnancy, maternity and paternity' have been included as examples of sex discrimination; 'civil partnership status' has been included as an example of sexual orientation discrimination; and age has been included in the list of the grounds that may give rise to discrimination.

Note 4 indicates that although the provisions of rule 6 are based upon legislative provisions, in a number of areas the rule goes beyond the scope of the legislation, in particular in relation to age discrimination. The law dealing with age discrimination currently applies only in relation to employment and vocational training; 6.01(1) applies to all of a lawyer's professional dealings.

Rule 6.01(2) introduces a provision relating to the disabled. This provides:

> You must take such steps, and make such adjustments, as are reasonable in all the circumstances in order to prevent any of your employees, partners, members, directors or clients who are disabled from being placed at a substantial disadvantage in comparison with those who are not disabled.

There is an important distinction to be made between the obligations contained in 6.01(1) (duty not to discriminate) and 6.01(2) (reasonable adjustment for disability). Rule 6.01(1) applies to all professional dealings (including those with any third parties), whereas 6.01(2) is restricted in its application to clients, employees, and the firm's managers (see note 4).

Significant guidance on the requirements of 6.01 can be found in the notes. In particular:

- the scope of the rule (notes 2–5);
- the meaning of discrimination (notes 6–10);
- permitted exceptions and justifiable discrimination (notes 11–13);
- dealing with clients and third parties (notes 14–18);
- partners and partnerships (notes 19–20).

EVIDENCE OF BREACH (6.02)

Rule 6.02 provides that a decision of a court or tribunal of the UK that an unlawful act of discrimination has been committed by a person bound by the rule shall be treated as evidence of a breach of rule 6. However, note 21 indicates that it will still be necessary for the SRA or the Solicitors Disciplinary Tribunal to determine whether a finding of discrimination amounts to professional misconduct.

EQUALITY AND DIVERSITY POLICY (6.03)

Rule 6.03 requires a recognised body, a manager of a recognised body or a recognised sole practitioner to adopt and implement an appropriate policy for preventing discrimination and harassment and promoting equality and diversity within their firm. All reasonable steps must be taken to ensure that all employees, partners, members and directors are aware of and act in compliance with its provisions and that it is made available to clients, the SRA and other relevant third parties where required.

You should note that there is no longer a model policy issued by the Law Society which will apply in default of a firm implementing its own policy. All firms must adopt and implement their own specific equality and diversity policy which is appropriate to the nature and size of the firm. Note 22 provides guidance upon what will be 'appropriate'. The note states:

To be appropriate the policy must:

(i) be in writing;
(ii) include such provisions as are relevant to your firm (having regard to its nature and size);
(iii) as a minimum, deal with the following core items:

   (A) how the firm plans to implement, communicate, monitor, evaluate and update the policy;
   (B) how the firm intends to ensure equality in relation to employees, managers, clients and third parties and the means by which it will monitor, evaluate and update any procedures and policies in relation to this;
   (C) how complaints and disciplinary issues are to be dealt with;
   (D) a requirement that all employees and managers comply with the provisions set out in 6.01; and
   (E) a commitment to the principles of equality and diversity and to observing legislative requirements;

(iv) not contain any additional items which would conflict with the core items.

The Law Society's Model Anti-Discrimination Policy was published in September 2004. Many firms of solicitors allowed the default provisions noted above to apply to their practices and were thus deemed to be bound by the model policy.

Practitioners may use the model policy as a starting point to develop their own policy but they must appreciate the fact that the model policy does not satisfy, in all ways, the requirement for an 'appropriate policy' necessary under 6.03. The model policy is still available on the SRA's website under 'archived rules' (see **www.tinyurl.com/cjnc3b**).

Practitioners must ensure that they address the need for an appropriate policy; that such a policy is in writing; that it contains, as a minimum, the points covered in note 22; and that it is brought to the attention of all managers and employees. Note 22(c)(ii) states that a policy which is not brought to the attention of such individuals will not be an appropriate policy.

In-house lawyers will not have the opportunity to formulate and implement discrimination policies in the same way as a manager or sole practitioner in private practice will have. However, 6.04 requires in-house lawyers with management responsibilities to use all reasonable endeavours to secure the adoption and implementation of an appropriate policy and requires them to take reasonable steps to ensure that all staff in their department are aware of and act in accordance with the policy.

Finally, it should be noted that the SRA has no power to waive any of the provisions of rule 6 (6.05).

CONCLUSION

The 2009 Amendment Rules do not really make any significant changes to the obligations contained in rule 6. However, the scope of many of the obligations is extended to cover all employees and all managers (whether they are lawyers or not). The following checklist may be used to ensure proper compliance with the rule.

Duty not to discriminate

- Ensure all employees and managers are aware of the duty and in particular are aware of the examples of some types of discrimination contained in rule 6.
- Adopt (if necessary) an appropriate policy to prevent disabled employees, members or clients from being placed at a substantial disadvantage (6.01(2)).

Equality and diversity policy

- If necessary adopt a new written policy (or make appropriate amendments to existing policies where necessary).
- Ensure the policy contains, as a minimum, the requirements in the rule.
- Ensure all employees and managers have a copy of the new policy.
- Consider including clauses in employment contracts and the partnership deed requiring compliance with the policy.

CHAPTER 7

Publicity

INTRODUCTION

Rule 7 deals with publicity.

The rule provides that you are generally free to publicise your practice but the rule does contain specific restrictions relating to publicity.

The rule covers the following topics:

- Misleading or inaccurate publicity
- Clarity as to charges
- Unsolicited approaches in person or by telephone
- International aspects of publicity
- Responsibility for publicity
- Application
- Letterhead, website and e-mails

SCOPE

Rule 7 applies to:

- solicitors or RELs practising from offices in England and Wales (including recognised sole practitioners practising as solicitors or RELs);
- recognised bodies (all practices other than recognised sole practitioners must now be recognised bodies);
- any other person who is a manager or employee of a recognised body or the employee of a recognised sole practitioner practising from offices in England and Wales;
- any RFL practising from offices in England and Wales as an employee of a recognised sole practitioner; a manager, employee, owner or director of a recognised body; or as a manager, member or owner of a body corporate which is a manager, member or owner of a recognised body.

Rule 7 generally applies to overseas practices except in relation to the website, e-mails, text messages or similar electronic communications of any practice you conduct from an office in an EU state other than the UK.

Further, 7.07 (Letterhead, website and e-mails) does not apply to overseas practices but if an REL is named on the notepaper, there must be compliance with 15.07(3)(a).

Rule 7 does not apply to solicitors, RELs or RFLs practising through or employed by a non-SRA authorised firm.

MISLEADING OR INACCURATE PUBLICITY (7.01)

The provisions of 7.01 provide that publicity must not be misleading or inaccurate. 'Publicity' is defined in rule 24 as including:

> all promotional material and activity, including the name or description of your firm, stationery, advertisements, brochures, websites, directory entries, media appearances, promotional press releases, and direct approaches to potential clients and other persons, whether conducted in person, in writing, or in electronic form, but does not include press releases prepared on behalf of a client.

Although rule 7 does not contain specific obligations relating to the name of the firm, by this definition requirements relating to the firm name are incorporated into the requirements of 7.01. Guidance notes 14 and 15 provide additional assistance regarding the name of the firm.

Note 5 sets out the statutory requirements affecting advertising and confirms that there must be compliance with the general law. Note 6 reminds practitioners that they must have regard to the British Code of Advertising, Sales Promotion and Direct Marketing and note 7 indicates that a breach of a statutory provision or the Advertising Code may give rise to a breach of rule 7.

CLARITY AS TO CHARGES (7.02)

Rule 7.02 requires publicity relating to charges to be clearly expressed. Notes 9–12 provide assistance in complying with these provisions.

UNSOLICITED APPROACHES IN PERSON OR BY TELEPHONE (7.03)

Rule 7.03 was amended by the Solicitors' (Cold Calling) Amendment Rule 2009 which came into effect on 14 January 2009 along with a new guidance note (note 30). The original provisions of 7.03 applied to unsolicited visits or calls. However the amended version makes it clear that unsolicited approaches in person are prohibited by the rule. The guidance note (note 30) gives examples of such prohibited approaches including 'knocking on doors, approaching people newly arrived at ports of entry, approaching someone in the street, in a hospital or at the scene of an accident, or handing out leaflets in the street. The rule also prohibits approaching a member of the public (either in person, e.g. in the street, or by telephone) to conduct a survey which involves the collection of contact details of potential clients, or otherwise promotes your firm's practice'.

It should be noted that as well as complying with the rule, practitioners who have financial arrangements with introducers (see rule 9 – Chapter 9 below) must be satisfied that any business introduced as a result of the arrangement has not been acquired as a result of marketing or publicity in breach of rule 7.

The prohibition on unsolicited approaches in person or by telephone applies where the publicity is addressed to a 'member of the public'. A 'member of the public' does not include (7.03(2)) a current or former client; another firm or its manager; an existing or potential professional or business connection or a commercial organisation or public body. Approaches to such individuals or businesses continue to be permitted by the Code (7.03) subject to the other provisions of the Code, in particular the core duties in rule 1. Any unsolicited approach in person or by telephone made to any other potential client would be prohibited.

Note 22 points out that this rule does not apply to e-mail (nor does it apply to any other written material that may be sent unsolicited – note 29). However, note 22 indicates that practitioners should check with their internet service provider before sending unsolicited e-mail and warns that unsolicited e-mail is prohibited by law in some jurisdictions.

Practitioners sending unsolicited mailshots or making unsolicited calls or visits should also consider the requirements of the Data Protection Act 1998 and the Electronic Communications (EC Directive) Regulations 2003 (SI 2003/2426) (see note 33 and below).

INTERNATIONAL ASPECTS OF PUBLICITY (7.04)

Rule 7.04 confirms that publicity intended for a jurisdiction outside England and Wales must comply with rule 7 of the Code and the rules of the jurisdiction concerning lawyers' publicity. (If the publicity is conducted from an overseas office, the requirements of 15.07 will also apply.)

Notes 16–21 provide guidance on the Electronic Commerce (EC Directive) Regulations 2002 (SI 2002/2013) which cover cross-border e-commerce within the EU. Cross-border e-commerce will include, for example:

- the e-publicity of a solicitor's overseas office established in the EU; or
- the e-publicity of firms practising in England and Wales if it is accessed or received in the EU.

The regulations impose an obligation to provide certain information in cross-border e-publicity and therefore may apply to cross-border e-mail correspondence and will inevitably apply to any firm with a website, because websites can be accessed from other member countries.

Notes 25–28 confirm that, as a result of the E-Commerce Directive 2000/31/ EC, there are two different regimes governing international e-publicity. Cross-border e-publicity will be governed by the Directive; other international e-publicity will not.

RESPONSIBILITY FOR PUBLICITY (7.05)

Rule 7.05 provides that other persons must not be authorised to conduct publicity on behalf of a practice in any way which would breach the requirements of rule 7. Note 8 provides guidance on the approach to take when a practitioner becomes aware of a breach by a third party – reasonable steps must be taken to have the publicity changed or withdrawn.

APPLICATION (7.06)

Rule 7.06(1) states that, where it applies, rule 7 imposes obligations relating to publicity you or your firm conduct or authorise in the course of setting up or carrying on practice in relation to:

- the firm or your practice;
- any other business or activity carried on by you or your firm; or
- any other business or activity carried on by others.

The 2009 Amendment Rules have amended rule 7.06 to make it clear that the rule applies to publicity conducted or authorised in the course of setting up or carrying on the practice. Consequently you must comply with the rule in relation to any publicity undertaken prior to the commencement of practice but where you are in the course of setting up practice.

Rule 7.06(2) states:

Rules 7.01 to 7.05 apply to all forms of publicity including the name or description of your firm, stationery, advertisements, brochures, websites, directory entries, media appearances, promotional press releases, and direct approaches to potential clients and other persons, and whether conducted in person, in writing, or in electronic form.

LETTERHEAD, WEBSITE AND E-MAILS (7.07)

The 2009 Amendment Rules extend some of the requirements of rule 7.07 to the firm's website and e-mails. The original rule only applied to 'letterheads' and the notes confirmed that since e-mails do not normally have letterheads 7.07 would not normally apply to e-mail. However as a result of the Amendment Rules practitioners must ensure that not only their letterheads but their websites and e-mails comply with the appropriate requirements. Further, 7.07(5) confirms that 'letterhead' includes a fax heading.

By 7.07(1) the letterhead, website and e-mails of a recognised body or recognised sole practitioner must show the words 'regulated by the Solicitors Regulation Authority'. In addition such letterheads, websites and e-mails must show:

- the firm's registered name and number if it is an LLP or company; or
- if the firm is a partnership or sole practitioner, the name under which it is recognised by the SRA and the number allocated to it by the SRA.

The additional obligations are new and as a result of the 2009 Amendment Rules. Consequently all practitioners must take steps to ensure that their letterhead, website and e-mails comply with the original obligation relating to regulation by the SRA and also include the additional disclosure requirements dependent upon the firm being an LLP, company, partnership or sole practitioner.

However, the requirements for a partnership, LLP or company to have on their website and e-mails the words 'regulated by the Solicitors Regulation Authority' and the obligation for a partnership to have on their letterhead, website and e-mails the name under which it is regulated and the number allocated by the SRA do not apply until 1 October 2009 (see 25.01(7)). Further, the requirements for registered sole practitioners to have on their website and e-mails the words 'regulated by the Solicitors Regulation Authority' and the obligation for them to have on their letterhead, website and e-mails the name under which they are regulated and the number allocated by the SRA do not apply until 1 January 2010.

The obligations relating to the disclosure of ownership information on the letterhead are set out in 7.07(2)–(5). Rule 7.07(2)–(5) only applies to letterheads and fax headings. It does not apply to the website or generally to e-mails. However the amended guidance note 21 states:

> Rule 7.07(2)–(4), which applies only to letterheads and fax headings, reflects some of the provisions of the Business Names Act 1985 and the Companies (Trading Disclosures) Regulations 2008, which apply to 'business letters'. It is for the courts to determine whether or to what extent these Acts may apply to e-mails. However, the SRA's guess is that e-mails will only be 'business letters' when they are formally set out as such and not when they are used as an alternative to a telephone call, telegram or telex. It would be prudent for you to ensure that third parties with whom you deal by e-mail are given your practising address at an early stage, together with the details which would normally appear on the firm's letterhead.

Rule 7.07(2) covers the position regarding the naming of sole practitioners, partners, members or directors on the letterhead of:

- a recognised sole practitioner;
- recognised bodies which are partnerships;
- recognised bodies which are LLPs;
- recognised bodies which are companies.

In defined circumstances, a statement that a list of names of partners, members or directors is open to inspection at the office can be shown in substitution for names. The position where the recognised body has managers other than solicitors is covered by 7.07(3). In any list referred to, solicitors must be identified as 'solicitors'; lawyers or notaries of an Establishment Directive state (other than the UK) must identify their professional title and jurisdiction under whose professional title the lawyer or notary is practising; any other lawyer must identify their professional qualification; individual non-lawyers must be identified as such; and any body corporate must identify its nature if this is not clear from its name.

Detailed guidance notes on 7.07 can be found in notes 34–43. In particular guidance can be found on:

- naming non-partners (note 34);
- salaried partners (note 35);
- 'partners' in an LLP (notes 36–39);
- 'partners' in a company (notes 40–42);
- managers and RELs (note 43).

OTHER GUIDANCE

In addition to the guidance noted above, the following guidance is provided:

- local law society involvement in dealing with minor breaches (note 3);
- financial promotions (notes 31–32);
- naming staff (notes 44 and 45);
- naming clients (note 46);
- fee earner leaving a firm (note 47).

CONCLUSION

The Cold Calling Amendment Rules and the 2009 Amendment Rules make some important changes to rule 7. Practitioners must ensure that their procedures relating to marketing and publicity are updated to comply with these changes. In particular:

- Ensure any cold calling (in person or by telephone) is permitted in the light of greater restrictions being imposed by the Cold Calling Amendment Rules.
- Ensure that third party introducers with whom the firm has financial arrangements are made aware of the new restrictions on cold calling and abide by them in relation to business introduced to the firm.
- Review the firm's letterhead, website and e-mail to ensure proper compliance with the amended rule 7.07(1) by 1 October 2009 (for partnerships, LLPs and companies) or by 1 January 2010 (for recognised sole practitioners).
- Review the list of the firm's partners, members or directors to ensure proper compliance with the amended rule 7.07(2)–(5).

CHAPTER 8

Fee sharing

INTRODUCTION

Rule 8 restricts the sharing of professional fees. It broadly prohibits the sharing of fees with a non-lawyer unless the non-lawyer is an employee or a manager of the firm. There are other exceptions set out in the rule. Fee sharing is not defined but note 1 to rule 8 provides that it may arise in a variety of forms including payment made by reference to:

- a percentage of fees charged to a client;
- a percentage of gross fees;
- a percentage of net fees; or
- a percentage of profits.

The rule covers the following topics:

- Fee sharing with lawyers and colleagues
- Fee sharing with other non-lawyers

SCOPE

Rule 8 applies to:

- solicitors or RELs practising from offices in England and Wales (including recognised sole practitioners practising as solicitors or RELs);
- recognised bodies (all practices other than recognised sole practitioners must now be recognised bodies);
- any other person who is a manager or employee of a recognised body or the employee of a recognised sole practitioner practising from offices in England and Wales;
- any RFL practising from offices in England and Wales as an employee of a recognised sole practitioner; a manager, employee, owner or director of a recognised body; or as a manager, member or owner of a body corporate which is a manager, member or owner of a recognised body.

Rule 8 applies in full to overseas practice (15.08).

Rule 8 does not apply to solicitors, RELs or RFLs practising through or employed by a non-SRA authorised firm.

FEE SHARING WITH LAWYERS AND COLLEAGUES (8.01)

The persons you can share or agree to share your professional fees with (subject to the exception in 8.02) are listed in eight categories (8.01(a)–(h)) as follows:

(a) practising lawyers, and businesses carrying on the practice of lawyers;

(b) non-lawyer managers or owners within your firm;

(c) a retired manager, member, owner or predecessor, or the dependants or personal representatives of a deceased manager, member, owner or predecessor;

(d) your genuine employee (this does not allow you to disguise as 'employment' what is in fact a partnership which rule 12 prohibits);

(e) your non-lawyer employer, if you are practising in-house and acting in accordance with rule 13 (In-house practice, etc.) or 15.13 (In-house practice overseas);

(f) a law centre or advice service operated by a charitable or similar non-commercial organisation if you are working as a volunteer and receive fees or costs from public funds or recovered from a third party; or

(g) an estate agent who is your sub-agent for the sale of a property; or

(h) a charity ... [subject to specified conditions].

FEE SHARING WITH OTHER NON-LAWYERS (8.02)

Fee sharing with a number of non-lawyers who are colleagues and charities is permitted by 8.01 – see, for example, 8.01(b) (non-lawyer managers); 8.01(d) (genuine employees); 8.01(e) (employers where the practice is in-house); 8.01(f) (law centres or advice centres); 8.01(g) (estate agents who are sub-agents) and 8.01(h) (charities).

Fee sharing with other persons or businesses who are not lawyers or colleagues is permitted by 8.02, provided certain conditions are satisfied. This exception to the general rule was first introduced in 2004 and limits the fee sharing to those arrangements which are solely to facilitate:

- the introduction of capital; and/or
- the provision of services.

In addition you must be satisfied that neither the fee sharing agreement nor the extent of the fees shared permits any fee sharer to influence or constrain your professional judgement in relation to any advice given to a client and the arrangement must not result in a partnership prohibited by rule 12 (see Chapter 12 below). If requested, details of all fee sharing agreements under 8.02 together with the percentage of the firm's annual gross fees which have been shared must be supplied to the SRA.

Guidance

Note 12 gives examples of the kind of arrangements permitted by 8.02. Note 13 states that although there is no specified cap or limit on the amount of fees that may be shared in accordance with 8.02, a risk assessment should be undertaken to ensure there is no breach of rule 1 (Core duties) as a result of the agreement. The SRA may ask for evidence of this risk assessment particularly where the percentage of all fees shared is higher than 15 per cent of the gross fees. See also note 7 to rule 1 regarding core duty 1.03 (Independence) (see Chapter 1 above).

CONCLUSION

The 2009 Amendment Rules have amended rule 8 to permit fee sharing within the new forms of practice permitted by the Legal Services Act 2007, notably LDPs. No other change of substance has been made.

CHAPTER 9

Referrals of business

INTRODUCTION

Rule 9 applies to referrals of business received from or made to third parties. It includes the conditions that will apply when there is a financial arrangement with the introducer. In relation to European cross-border practice the restrictions on financial arrangements with introducers are more stringent. These are dealt with in rule 16 (see Chapter 16 below).

The following topics are covered by rule 9:

- General principles
- Financial arrangements with introducers
- Referrals to third parties

SCOPE

Rule 9 applies to:

- solicitors or RELs practising from offices in England and Wales (including recognised sole practitioners practising as solicitors or RELs);
- recognised bodies (all practices other than recognised sole practitioners must now be recognised bodies);
- any other person who is a manager or employee of a recognised body or the employee of a recognised sole practitioner practising from offices in England and Wales;
- any RFL practising from offices in England and Wales as an employee of a recognised sole practitioner; a manager, employee, owner or director of a recognised body; or as a manager, member or owner of a body corporate which is a manager, member or owner of a recognised body.

Rule 9 does not apply to overseas practice but 15.09 reminds practitioners that when practising overseas they are subject to the core duties and other applicable provisions of the Code. Further, rule 16 (European cross-border practice) prohibits payments for referrals to non-lawyers when undertaking cross-border activities (see Chapter 16 below).

Rule 8 does not apply to solicitors, RELs or RFLs practising through or employed by a non-SRA authorised firm.

GENERAL (9.01)

Rule 9.01 sets out the general principles applicable when you receive referrals from or make referrals to third parties. It covers the following points.

All referrals must be made or received without compromising independence or the ability to act in the best interests of the client (9.01(1))

Rule 9 does not impose a formal record keeping requirement and unlike the earlier rules on referrals, there is no longer a strict obligation to conduct six-monthly reviews. However, guidance note 1 recommends that firms do conduct regular reviews of referral arrangements to ensure that over-reliance on an introducer does not affect the advice given to clients. Factors that should be considered in such a review include:

- whether there has been compliance with the provisions of rule 9;
- whether referred clients have been given independent advice, unaffected by the interests of the introducer; and
- the amount and proportion of the firm's income arising as a result of each referral arrangement.

While a formal review is no longer mandatory, principals of firms should adopt some appropriate procedure to ensure proper compliance with the rule.

Potential introducers must be informed of the provisions of rule 9 and rule 7 (9.01(2))

In the light of the amendments to rule 7 relating to unsolicited approaches in person or by telephone (see Chapter 7 above) it is vital that potential introducers are made aware of these amendments to ensure that practitioners comply with 9.01(2).

Rule 9 does not apply to referrals between lawyers (9.01(3))

A lawyer is defined in rule 24 as:

a member of one of the following professions, entitled to practise as such:

(a) the profession of solicitor, barrister or advocate of the UK;

(b) a profession whose members are authorised to practise by an approved regulator other than the Solicitors Regulation Authority;

(c) an Establishment Directive profession other than a UK profession;

(d) a legal profession which has been approved by the Solicitors Regulation Authority for the purpose of recognised bodies in England and Wales; or

(e) any other regulated legal profession which is recognised as such by the Solicitors Regulation Authority; ...

Consequently, the payment of referral fees between lawyers will not give rise to the obligation to comply with rule 9. Obviously, however, where there are referrals between lawyers other rules may be appropriate, e.g. rule 1 (Core duties), rule 2.06 (Commissions) and rule 7 (Publicity).

Prohibition on arrangements with third parties who solicit or receive contingency fees in respect of claims arising as a result of death or personal injury (9.01(4))

Rule 9.01(4) imposes a prohibition on entering into arrangements or acting in association with certain third parties in respect of any claim arising out of death or personal injury. However, 9.01(5) excludes the prohibition in 9.01(4) from applying to proceedings undertaken in a country other than England and Wales and where a local lawyer in that country would be permitted to receive a contingency fee in respect of such proceedings.

'Contingency fee' for the purpose of 9.01(4) and (5) is defined in 9.01(6) as:

> any sum (whether fixed, or calculated either as a percentage of the proceeds or otherwise howsoever) payable only in the event of success in the prosecution or defence of any action, suit or other contentious proceedings.

This is different from the definition of contingency fees to be found in rule 24 (Interpretation) and used in rule 2 (Client relations – see above, Chapter 2). The reason for the difference is that in rule 2 the prohibition on entering into an arrangement to receive a contingency fee (defined for this purpose as 'any sum ... payable only in the event of success') only applies to certain contentious proceedings and is subject to an exception where such a fee is permitted by statute or the common law. Thus rule 2 allows solicitors to enter into conditional fee agreements, which are a form of contingency fee permitted by statute. Rule 9 prohibits solicitors from having arrangements with third parties who solicit or receive contingency fees. The different definition of contingency fees for the purpose of rule 9 means that the prohibition applies to 'any action, suit or other contentious proceedings' and there is no exception for any possible statutory or common law contingency fee.

FINANCIAL ARRANGEMENTS WITH INTRODUCERS (9.02)

Rule 9.02 permits financial arrangements with introducers subject to conditions. Rule 9.02(i) defines 'financial arrangement' for these purposes and the term covers a payment made to an introducer in return for the introduction of a client or where an introducer pays the solicitor for legal services provided to the introducer's customer. 'Payment' is also defined in 9.02(i) as including any 'other consideration' but does not include normal hospitality, proper disbursements or normal business expenses. Further guidance on 'other consideration' can be found in note 5. Guidance on 'normal hospitality' can be found in note 15 and on 'normal business expenses' in note 16.

A number of points need to be made regarding the application of 9.02:

- 9.02(a): The agreement must be in writing and be available for inspection by the SRA.
- 9.02(b): In all circumstances where there are financial arrangements with introducers, the introducer must undertake, as part of the agreement, to comply with the provisions of the rule.
- 9.02(c) requires you to be satisfied that clients referred by an introducer have not been acquired as a result of publicity or marketing which would breach the Code if undertaken by a person regulated by the SRA. Further guidance can be found in notes 11 and 12. Note also the amendments to rule 7 (7.03 – Unsolicited approaches in person or by telephone) (see Chapter 7 above). You must be satisfied that the introducer has not acquired clients through activities which would breach these new provisions.
- 9.02(d) prohibits certain terms in the agreement that would compromise the solicitor's duties or constrain the solicitor's professional judgement. Guidance can be found in note 13.
- 9.02(e) requires certain information to be given to the client by the introducer before making the referral. The information covers the situation where there is a referral fee paid by the solicitor or where the introducer is paying the solicitor for services provided to the introducer's customers.

In particular the information concerning the referral which must be given by the introducer must include the following:

(i)   the fact that the introducer has a financial arrangement with you; and
(ii) the amount of any payment to the introducer which is calculated by reference to that referral; or
(iii) where the introducer is paying you to provide services to the introducer's customers:

    (A) the amount the introducer is paying you to provide those services; and
    (B) the amount the client is required to pay the introducer.

Guidance on the disclosure of the amount of payment can be found in notes 6 and 7.

- 9.02(f) covers the requirements where there is reason to believe the introducer is breaching the terms of the agreement.
- 9.02(g) requires you to give certain information to the client in writing before accepting instructions to act where there has been a referral under 9.02 (i.e. where there are financial arrangements with an introducer). Note

9 provides guidance on the timing of the disclosure. This information is in addition to the information required to be given under rule 2. All relevant information concerning the referral must be supplied and in particular the following:

(i) the fact that you have a financial arrangement with the introducer;

(ii) the amount of any payment to the introducer which is calculated by reference to that referral; or

(iii) where the introducer is paying you to provide services to the introducer's customers:

(A) the amount the introducer is paying you to provide those services; and

(B) the amount the client is required to pay the introducer;

(iv) a statement that any advice you give will be independent and that the client is free to raise questions on all aspects of the transaction; and

(v) confirmation that information disclosed to you by the client will not be disclosed to the introducer unless the client consents; but that where you are also acting for the introducer in the same matter and a conflict of interests arises, you might be obliged to cease acting.

Guidance on the disclosure of the amount of payment can be found in notes 6 and 7.

- 9.02(h) gives details of the excepted matters where financial arrangements with introducers are not permitted (criminal proceedings and publicly funded work). Note 14 provides further guidance.

REFERRALS TO THIRD PARTIES (9.03)

Rule 9.03 sets out the obligations where you refer clients to a third party. The requirements are:

- referrals must be in good faith;
- no agreement can restrict your freedom to recommend any particular third party;
- where the client is likely to need an endowment policy or other insurance product with an investment element, the referral must be to an authorised and independent intermediary.

The Code recognises that under the Solicitors' Financial Services (Scope) Rules 2001 it is possible for solicitors to provide advice on certain insurance products and to limit their advice to products from a limited number of providers. Further, under the Financial Services and Markets Act 2000 (Regulated Activities) Order 2001 (SI 2001/544) it is possible for solicitors to introduce clients to authorised lenders in respect of regulated mortgage contracts.

Notes 17–19 provide further guidance.

CONCLUSION

The 2009 Amendment Rules make no changes of substance to rule 9. However, there is evidence that many firms breach rule 9 in respect of financial arrangements they have with introducers and the SRA has issued 'Referrals Warning Guidance' indicating that it is 'cracking down' on improper referrals and increasing the number of regulatory visits to firms.

CHAPTER 10

Relations with third parties

INTRODUCTION

Rule 10 brings together a number of obligations relating to dealing with third parties. Third parties for the purpose of this rule include clients, lawyers (e.g. solicitors, barristers, overseas lawyers), professional and other agents and members of the public. The following topics are dealt with in rule 10:

- Not taking unfair advantage
- Agreeing costs with another party
- Administering oaths
- Contacting other party to a matter
- Undertakings
- Dealing with more than one prospective buyer in a conveyancing transaction
- Fees of lawyers of other jurisdictions

SCOPE

Rule 10 applies to:

- solicitors or RELs practising from offices in England and Wales (including recognised sole practitioners practising as solicitors or RELs);
- recognised bodies (all practices other than recognised sole practitioners must now be recognised bodies);
- any other person who is a manager or employee of a recognised body or the employee of a recognised sole practitioner practising from offices in England and Wales;
- an RFL practising from offices in England and Wales as an employee of a recognised sole practitioner; a manager, employee, owner or director of a recognised body; or as a manager, member or owner of a body corporate which is a manager, member or owner of a recognised body.

While rule 10 does apply generally to overseas practice, 15.10 provides that the rule dealing with undertakings (10.05) does not apply to overseas practice. However 15.10(2) does impose some limited obligations relating to undertakings given overseas as follows:

- Undertakings must be fulfilled if given:
    - in the course of practice;
    - outside the course of practice but as a 'solicitor'; or
    - outside the course of practice as a lawyer of an Establishment Directive profession by an REL based in an office in Scotland or Northern Ireland.
- Undertakings must be fulfilled within a reasonable time.
- If an undertaking is given which is dependent on the happening of a future event the recipient must be notified immediately if it becomes clear the event will not occur.

Further, 15.10(3) makes it clear that 10.06 (Dealing with more than one prospective buyer in a conveyancing transaction) applies only if the land is situated in England and Wales.

Rule 10 does not apply to solicitors, RELs or RFLs practising through or employed by a non-SRA authorised firm when doing work of a sort authorised by the firm's approved regulator.

NOT TAKING UNFAIR ADVANTAGE (10.01)

It is specifically stated later in the Code, rule 23.02 (Application) that 10.01 applies in relation to activities in England and Wales which fall outside the scope of practice whether undertaken as a lawyer or in some other business or private capacity if you are a solicitor, or REL. In this context 'practice' is defined as the activities of a solicitor, in that capacity and the activities of an REL in the capacity of a lawyer of an Establishment Directive profession from an office within the UK.

Notes 1–6 provide guidance on 10.01. In particular, note 1 gives an illustration of how the rule might apply to a solicitor's behaviour outside practice. The notes also cover:

- dealing with unrepresented or unqualified persons (notes 2 and 3);
- the inappropriate use of the title 'solicitor' (note 4);
- demanding anything that is not recoverable through the proper legal process (note 5);
- documents or money received subject to an express condition (note 6(a));
- documents or money received and held to the sender's order (note 6(b));
- payment of a proper charge where you request anyone to supply copy documents (note 6(c)).

AGREEING COSTS WITH ANOTHER PARTY (10.02)

Where you are negotiating the payment of your costs by a third party, 10.02 requires you to give sufficient time and information for the amount of your costs to be agreed and assessed. Notes 7 and 8 provide guidance on 10.02.

ADMINISTERING OATHS (10.03)

Rule 10.03 confirms that those who are subject to the Code and who are authorised to do so may administer oaths or affirmations and can take declarations. It imposes a restriction where you or your firm are 'acting for any party in the matter'. This makes it clear that the restriction can apply to any retainer. This restriction is based upon the Solicitors Act 1974, s.81(2). Guidance notes 9–13 cover the following matters:

- who is authorised to administer oaths, etc. (note 9);
- your responsibilities when administering oaths, etc. (note 10);
- responsibility for contents of the document (note 11);
- prohibition on administering an oath, etc. (note 12);
- pre-signed oaths (note 13).

CONTACTING OTHER PARTY TO A MATTER (10.04)

Rule 10.04 prohibits you from communicating with any other party who, to your knowledge, has retained a lawyer or a business carrying on the practice of lawyers, to act in a matter. 'Lawyer' means (rule 24):

a member of one of the following professions, entitled to practise as such:

(a) the profession of solicitor, barrister or advocate of the UK;
(b) a profession whose members are authorised to practise by an approved regulator other than the Solicitors Regulation Authority;
(c) an Establishment Directive profession other than a UK profession;
(d) a legal profession which has been approved by the Solicitors Regulation Authority for the purpose of registered bodies in England and Wales; or
(e) any other regulated legal profession which is recognised as such by the Solicitors Regulation Authority; ...

Significant guidance on 10.04 is provided in notes 14–23.

UNDERTAKINGS (10.05)

Rule 24 defines an undertaking for the purpose of 10.05 as meaning:

a statement made by you or your firm to someone who reasonably relies upon it, that you or your firm will do something or cause something to be done, or refrain from doing something. The undertaking can be given orally or in writing and need not include the words 'undertake' or 'undertaking'.

The circumstances in which you must fulfil an undertaking are set out in 10.05(1) as follows:

(a) you give the undertaking in the course of practice;

(b) you are a recognised body, a manager of a recognised body or a recognised sole practitioner, and any person within the firm gives the undertaking in the course of practice;

(c) you give the undertaking outside the course of practice, but as a solicitor; or

(d) you are an REL based at an office in England and Wales, and you give the undertaking within the UK, as a lawyer of an Establishment Directive profession but outside your practice as an REL.

Note that 10.05(1)(d) extends the responsibility for fulfilling an undertaking to an REL outside practice as an REL in certain defined circumstances.

Rule 10.05 does not apply generally to overseas practice (15.10). However, 15.10(2) does impose some limited obligations relating to undertakings given overseas (for details, see 'Scope' above).

Undertakings must be fulfilled within a reasonable time (10.05(2)). Rule 10.05(3) deals with undertakings that are dependent upon the happening of a future event. You must notify the recipient immediately if it becomes clear that the event will not occur. Rule 10.05(4) deals with undertakings to pay another's costs and the circumstances when this may be discharged.

Notes 24–41 provide significant guidance on undertakings.

DEALING WITH MORE THAN ONE PROSPECTIVE BUYER IN A CONVEYANCING TRANSACTION (10.06)

Rule 10.06 applies where you are instructed by a seller of land (other than a sale by auction or tender) to deal with more than one prospective buyer. It also applies where, to your knowledge, the seller deals directly with another prospective buyer or their conveyancer or instructs another conveyancer to deal with the buyer. Note 42 gives guidance on the meaning of 'deal' for these purposes and confirms that providing information only as part of a Home Information Pack will not amount to dealing.

Rule 10.06 states that where you are instructed to deal with more than one prospective buyer (or the seller deals directly or instructs another conveyancer to deal with another buyer) you must 'inform' the conveyancer of each prospective buyer (or the buyer if acting in person). Note 44 states that you must inform by the most suitable means – if the information is given in person or by telephone there is no requirement that the details be confirmed in writing (although it is advisable to do so).

Rule 10.06(3) provides that you cannot act for the seller and any of the prospective buyers (this is so even if one of the exceptions (e.g. established clients) in 3.09 would seem to apply (see Chapter 3)). Further you cannot act for more than one prospective buyer.

Although 10.06 applies to overseas practice, 15.10 restricts the operation of 10.06 to where the land is situated in England and Wales.

FEES OF LAWYERS OF OTHER JURISDICTIONS (10.07)

Rule 10.07 applies where you instruct a lawyer of another jurisdiction (other than a lawyer practising overseas as a lawyer of England and Wales). Where the rule applies, you must, as a matter of professional conduct, pay the lawyer's proper fees.

Rule 10.07(1)(a) allows you to expressly disclaim the responsibility and provides that this disclaimer may be made at the outset (in which case there will be no responsibility for the lawyer's fees) or the disclaimer may be made at a later date (in which case there will be no responsibility for fees incurred after that date).

Note 46 distinguishes between instructing a foreign lawyer (when liability for their fees will arise if no exception applies) and introducing or referring a client to a foreign lawyer (when no liability for their fees will arise).

Further, 10.07 does not apply if:

- the lawyer is an REL or is registered with the Bar of England and Wales under the Establishment Directive; or
- the lawyer is an RFL based in England and Wales and practising in a firm.

Rule 10.07(2) imposes an obligation to pay the proper fees of a business carrying on the practice of a lawyer of another jurisdiction where you instruct that business unless:

- there is an express disclaimer; or
- the business is a firm (i.e. a business through which a solicitor or REL carries on practice other than in-house practice – see rule 24).

CONCLUSION

The 2009 Amendment Rules make no change of substance to rule 10 other than the scope of the rule being extended to non-lawyer managers and employees.

CHAPTER 11

Litigation and advocacy

INTRODUCTION

Rule 11 imposes obligations where a firm or a lawyer exercises the right to conduct litigation or when acting as an advocate. Guidance notes are included which cover topics outside the specific areas covered by the rule.

As noted above, the guidance notes technically do not form part of the Code. However, practitioners must remember that they are bound by the core duties, particularly 1.01 (Justice and the rule of law) which requires those bound by the Code to uphold the rule of law and the proper administration of justice. These core duties may require compliance with some of the topics covered in the guidance notes.

The following topics are covered by the rule and compliance with their provisions is thus mandatory:

- Deceiving or misleading the court
- Obeying court orders
- Contempt of court
- Refusing instructions to act as advocate
- Appearing as an advocate
- Appearing as a witness
- Payments to witnesses
- Recordings of child witnesses' evidence

General guidance (as opposed to specific guidance on the mandatory topics in rule 11) can be found on the followings matters:

- best interests of the client (note 5);
- obligations as an officer of the court, consistent with the duties owed to a client (note 6);
- communication with judges outside the courtroom (note 7);
- standing bail for clients (note 8);
- attending advocates at court (notes 9 and 10);
- statements to the media (note 11).

SCOPE

Rule 11 applies to:

- solicitors or RELs practising from offices in England and Wales (including recognised sole practitioners practising as solicitors or RELs);
- recognised bodies (all practices other than recognised sole practitioners must now be recognised bodies);
- any other person who is a manager or employee of a recognised body or the employee of a recognised sole practitioner practising from offices in England and Wales;
- any RFL practising from offices in England and Wales as an employee of a recognised sole practitioner; a manager, employee, owner or director of a recognised body; or as a manager, member or owner of a body corporate which is a manager, member or owner of a recognised body.

Notes 1–4 provide guidance on the entitlement of solicitors, RELs, RFLs and other lawyers to conduct litigation and exercise the right of audience. Generally only solicitors, RELs and certain other lawyers are entitled to conduct litigation or exercise rights of audience. RFLs and non-lawyers are only entitled to exercise rights which are not reserved by law to any category of persons but are open to any individual (subject to minor exceptions for RFLs – see note 3).

Rule 11 only applies to overseas offices in respect of litigation or advocacy conducted before a court, tribunal or inquiry in England and Wales or a British court martial. Rule 11 does not apply to litigation or advocacy conducted in another jurisdiction although the core duties will always apply in these circumstances.

Rule 11 does not apply to solicitors, RELs or RFLs practising through or employed by a non-SRA authorised firm when doing work of a sort authorised by the firm's approved regulator. However if, for example, a solicitor practises through a firm of licensed conveyancers and undertakes work of a sort not authorised by the Council for Licensed Conveyancers (e.g. litigation in the form of debt collecting for the firm) the solicitor will be 'practising from an office in England and Wales' and will thus be subject to rule 11. Note that solicitors, RELs and RFLs practising through or employed by a non-SRA authorised firm are generally restricted to undertaking work authorised by the firm's approved regulator (see rule 12 and Chapter 12 below) or undertaking other work for the firm itself or as permitted by rule 13 (see Chapter 13 below).

DECEIVING OR MISLEADING THE COURT (11.01)

You must never deceive or knowingly or recklessly mislead the court (11.01(1)). Court is defined for these purposes (rule 24) as 'any court, tribunal or enquiry of England and Wales, or a British court martial, or any court of another jurisdiction'. Although litigation or advocacy conducted from an overseas office in another jurisdiction is not subject to rule 11, litigation or advocacy conducted from an office in England and Wales in a court of another jurisdiction will be subject to rule 11.

Certain information must be drawn to the attention of the court (11.01(2)). This includes relevant cases and statutory provisions; the contents of any document that has been filed in the proceedings where failure to draw it to the court's attention might result in the court being misled; and any procedural irregularity. Notes 12–19 provide additional guidance on deceiving or misleading the court and in particular note 13 gives some illustrations of what might be considered to be a breach of 11.01.

OBEYING COURT ORDERS (11.02)

You must comply with any court order requiring you or your firm to take, or refrain from taking, any particular course of action. Note 20 gives further, limited guidance.

CONTEMPT OF COURT (11.03)

You must not become in contempt of court. New guidance was issued in January 2008 stating: 'You could, for example, become in contempt of court by making a statement to the press which is calculated to interfere with the fair trial of a case which has not been concluded' (note 21).

REFUSING INSTRUCTIONS TO ACT AS ADVOCATE (11.04)

Rule 2.01 (see Chapter 2) provides that you are generally free to decide whether or not to take on a particular client. Rule 11.04(1) restricts that right where you act as an advocate – it specifies the grounds on which you must not refuse to act as advocate. These are:

(a) that the nature of the case is objectionable to you or to any section of the public;
(b) that the conduct, opinions or beliefs of the prospective client are unacceptable to you or to any section of the public; or
(c) that the source of any financial support which may properly be given to the prospective client for the proceedings is unacceptable to you.

In addition to the three grounds specified in 11.04(1), note 22 reminds advocates that they must also comply with rule 6 (Equality and diversity).

You are not required to act as an advocate under a conditional fee agreement or where you are not being offered a proper fee (11.04(2)). Note 23 gives guidance on what is a proper fee in publicly funded matters.

APPEARING AS AN ADVOCATE (11.05)

This rule sets out a number of issues relating to the way in which you conduct yourself in court. Note 24 points out that there may be other restrictions, such as the rules of court, which affect the way a case may be presented.

APPEARING AS A WITNESS (11.06)

Rule 11.06 limits the circumstances where you can act as an advocate at a trial or act in litigation where you or anyone in your firm will be called as a witness. Notes 26–29 provide further guidance.

PAYMENTS TO WITNESSES (11.07)

Rule 11.07 prohibits the making of payments to a witness dependent upon the nature of the evidence given or upon the outcome of the case. However, note 30 provides that there is no objection to paying reasonable expenses to witnesses and reasonable compensation for loss of time attending court.

RECORDINGS OF CHILD WITNESSES' EVIDENCE (11.08)

Rule 11.08 imposes obligations where you are acting for either the defence or prosecution and you have a copy of an audio or video recording of a child witness in the circumstances covered by 11.08. The recommended form of undertaking is to be found in note 31 and other guidance appears in notes 32–34.

CONCLUSION

The 2009 Amendment Rules make no change of substance to rule 11 other than the scope of the rule being extended to non-lawyer managers and employees (which will be in limited circumstances only when they are entitled to exercise rights that are not reserved by law to any category of persons but are open to any individual).

CHAPTER 12

Framework of practice

INTRODUCTION

Rule 12 sets out the types of business through which solicitors, RELs, RFLs and recognised bodies may practise under the regulation of the SRA.

Significant amendments have been made as a result of the Legal Services Act 2007 and the 2009 Amendment Rules.

For most solicitors, rule 12 will be of little relevance to their day-to-day practice. Solicitors who are recognised sole practitioners, or partners or members of recognised bodies (partnerships formed under the law of England and Wales or limited liability partnerships) will be aware that their mode of practice is both common and permitted. In-house solicitors can be employed by a non-solicitor employer (which is not an authorised firm) providing they undertake work only for their employer or, in relation to other work, they comply with the requirements of rule 13. Rule 12 obviously allows such businesses.

Of necessity, the Code must address the framework of practice in circumstances where other lawyers are managers, employees, members or owners of recognised bodies (e.g. RELs, other lawyers or RFLs). Rule 12 covers the position of:

- Solicitors
- RELs
- RFLs
- Recognised bodies
- Managers and employees authorised by another approved regulator
- Managers and employees who are not lawyers

SCOPE

Rule 12 applies to:

- solicitors or RELs practising from offices in England and Wales (including recognised sole practitioners practising as solicitors or RELs);
- recognised bodies (all practices other than recognised sole practitioners must now be recognised bodies);

- any other person who is a manager or employee of a recognised body or the employee of a recognised sole practitioner practising from offices in England and Wales;
- any RFL practising from offices in England and Wales as an employee of a recognised sole practitioner; a manager, employee, owner or director of a recognised body; or as a manager, member or owner of a body corporate which is a manager, member or owner of a recognised body.

Rule 12 applies in full to overseas practice (15.12). Further, rule 12 applies to you if you are a solicitor, REL or RFL practising through or employed by an authorised non-SRA firm when doing work of a sort authorised by the firm's regulator. The definition of 'practising through' a non-SRA firm includes being a partner or member if the firm is a partnership or LLP or being a director or having an ownership interest if the body is a company and in neither case is it necessary for you to undertake work for the firm's clients (see rule 23 – Application of these rules).

SOLICITORS (12.01)

Rule 12.01 sets out the different ways in which solicitors can practise from:

- an office in England and Wales (12.01(1)); and
- an office outside England and Wales (12.01(2)).

To practise from an office in England and Wales a solicitor must fall within one of five categories set out in 12.01. 'Practice' means the activities of a solicitor in that capacity and 'practice from an office' includes practice carried on from an office in which the solicitor is based or from an office of a firm of which the solicitor is the sole principal or a manager or in which the solicitor has an ownership interest, even if not based there (rule 24).

The five categories in 12.01 are:

- A recognised sole practitioner or an employee of a recognised sole practitioner.
- A solicitor exempted from the obligation to be a recognised sole practitioner (rule 20.03 permits sole practice without recognition, for example, when practising as a locum or when providing services to family or friends free of charge).
- A manager, employee, member or owner of: a recognised body; or a company which is a manager, member or owner of a recognised body. The term 'manager' catches partners, members of LLPs and directors of companies. The reference to 'owner' would cover a shareholder of a company who was not a director (and thus not a 'manager'). 'Member' is included to cover a shareholder holding shares as a nominee (and thus not an 'owner').

- A manager, employee, member or owner of: an authorised non-SRA firm; or a company which is a manager, member or owner of an authorised non-SRA firm. In this case, solicitors are restricted to undertaking work authorised by the firm's approved regulator or undertaking other work for the firm itself or as permitted by rule 13 (see Chapter 13 below).
- An employee of another person, business or organisation. In this case solicitors are restricted to undertaking work only for the employer or as permitted by rule 13 (see Chapter 13 below).

Further guidance on these provisions can be found in notes 7–12.

To practise from an office outside England and Wales solicitors must fall within one of the five permitted categories in 12.01(2). The categories are:

- A sole practitioner. A sole practitioner practising only from outside England and Wales need not be recognised (see 20.03). A sole practitioner practising from an office in England and Wales and also overseas must be recognised.
- An employee of a sole principal who is a lawyer. A 'lawyer' is defined in rule 24 (see also 9.01(3) – Chapter 9).
- A manager, employee, member or owner of a recognised body. If any of the body's managers or owners are non-lawyers and the practice is in an Establishment Directive state (currently all EU states plus Iceland, Liechtenstein, Norway and Switzerland) the rules of that state for local lawyers must permit such a practice.
- A manager, employee, member or owner of a business that has no office in England and Wales. Such businesses must carry on the practice of law and the majority of the managers and owners (i.e. more than 50 per cent) must be lawyers. Further, if any owners or managers are non-lawyers and are subject to the rules for local lawyers, the business composition and structure must comply with those rules (in the case of any Establishment Directive state, in all cases even if there are no local lawyers in the firm; in other cases only if there are local lawyers in the firm).
- An employee of another person, business or organisation. In this case solicitors are restricted to undertaking work only for the employer or as permitted by rule 15.13 (see Chapter 15 below).

Further guidance can be found in notes 13–17.

RELS (12.02)

Rule 12.02 sets out the different ways in which RELs can practise from:

- an office in England and Wales (12.02(1)); and
- an office in Scotland or Northern Ireland (12.02(2)).

An REL can practise as an REL from an office in England and Wales but must do so in one of the same five categories of practice as a solicitor (see 12.01(1) above). The wording of 12.02(1) is the same as the wording in 12.01(1) save for the reference to 'REL' instead of 'solicitor'. Further, the same five categories of practice overseas contained in 12.01(2) apply with appropriate wording to RELs in 12.02(2) save for the fact that 12.02(2) only applies where RELs practise from an office in Scotland or Northern Ireland. Rule 12 does not apply to RELs practising from an office outside the UK.

RFLS (12.03)

Rule 12.03 sets out the different ways in which RFLs may practise:

- in their capacity as an RFL (12.03(1)); or
- in a capacity other than as an RFL (12.03(2)–(4)).

Rule 12.03(1) restricts practice as a foreign lawyer in the capacity of an RFL to three categories. These are:

- An employee of a recognised sole practitioner. An RFL is not entitled to practise as an RFL sole practitioner. Foreign lawyers may practise as sole practitioners but not as RFLs. Where an RFL practises in a capacity other than as an RFL the restrictions contained in 12.03(2) and (3) apply. Foreign lawyer sole practitioners who are not registered with the SRA are not subject to the Code but are subject to the general law with regard to the provision of any legal services. There is no requirement for a foreign lawyer to be registered in order to be employed by a recognised body or a recognised sole practitioner. Those who are registered will be subject to SRA regulation in respect of their capacity as an RFL. Non-registered foreign lawyers who are employees will be subject to the Code in the same way as other non-lawyer employees of recognised bodies and recognised sole practitioners.
- A manager, employee, member or owner of a recognised body or a company which is a manager, member or owner of a recognised body.
- A manager, employee, member or owner of an authorised non-SRA firm or a company which is a manager, member or owner of an authorised non-SRA firm. In this situation all the work undertaken by the RFL must be of the sort authorised by the non-SRA approved regulator or done for the firm itself or in accordance with rule 13 (see Chapter 13 below).

Registration as an RFL does not entitle the lawyer to practise as an in-house RFL. RFLs may provide in-house services (i.e. work for or be a principal or owner of an organisation that is neither a recognised body nor a non-SRA authorised firm) but in these circumstances will not be practising as an RFL. They will however, as RFLs, be subject to the restrictions contained in 12.03(2) and (3).

In all circumstances (i.e. whether or not practising as an RFL) RFLs will be subject to the further obligations relating to scope of practice to be found in 12.03(4) and (5).

Guidance for RFLs can be found in notes 21–29.

RECOGNISED BODIES (12.04)

Rule 12.04 applies to recognised bodies which must have at least one office in England and Wales (see rule 14 – Chapter 14 below).

Recognised bodies may practise from an office in England and Wales in one of four ways:

- as a stand-alone firm;
- as a manager, member or owner of another recognised body;
- as a manager, member or owner of an authorised non-SRA firm (providing the work undertaken by the body falls within the scope of the firm's authorisation);
- as an executor, trustee or nominee company or a company providing secretarial services, owned and operated by another recognised body or by a recognised sole practitioner.

The effect of rule 12 is that solicitors and RELs cannot provide services to the public in England and Wales except through a firm which is a recognised body or a recognised sole practitioner or an authorised non-SRA firm regulated by another approved regulator. Previously only incorporated practices were recognised bodies (i.e. companies and LLPs). Now all solicitor firms regulated by the SRA and providing services to the public in England and Wales must be recognised (including traditional partnerships and sole practitioners). Existing companies and LLPs at the date of commencement (31 March 2009) will, of necessity, already have recognised body status. All existing solicitor and REL partnerships as at 31 March will have been recognised by the SRA automatically. Existing sole practitioners will be recognised by the SRA in July 2009 and from the date of commencement of the amendments to the Code (31 March 2009) until then their recognition will be exempt from the need for recognition. Any new practice set up in the future will need to obtain recognised body status before commencing work.

Rule 12.04(2) sets out the ways in which a recognised body can practise from an office outside England and Wales.

Guidance on regulated bodies can be found in notes 30–37.

MANAGERS AND EMPLOYEES AUTHORISED BY ANOTHER APPROVED REGULATOR (12.05)

Rule 14 (Recognised bodies – see Chapter 14) allows managers (i.e. partners in a partnership, members of an LLP or directors of companies) of recognised bodies to be solicitors, RELs, RFLS and, inter alia, other lawyers of England and Wales. Rule 24 defines 'lawyers' for these purposes as those belonging to a profession whose members are authorised to practise by an approved regulator other than the Solicitors Regulation Authority. The 'approved regulators' (other than the SRA) listed in the Legal Services Act 2007, Sched.4 are:

- the General Council of the Bar (regulating barristers);
- the Master of the Faculties (regulating notaries);
- the Institute of Legal Executives (regulating legal executives);
- the Council for Licensed Conveyancers (regulating licensed conveyancers);
- the Chartered Institute of Patent Attorneys (regulating patent agents);
- the Institute of Trade Mark Attorneys (regulating trade mark attorneys);
- the Association of Law Costs Draftsmen (regulating law costs draftsmen).

Rule 12.05 imposes obligations on those lawyers of England and Wales who are managers or employees of recognised bodies or recognised sole practitioners who are not solicitors. The rule prohibits such lawyers from holding themselves out in any way which suggests that they are, or are entitled to practise as, a solicitor. The rule also imposes restrictions on the activities that can be undertaken by lawyers who are not solicitors, unless such restricted work is authorised by the lawyer's approved regulator or the work is undertaken under the supervision of (or in the case of advocacy in chambers, under instructions given by) a person qualified to direct reserved work.

Guidance on these provisions can be found in notes 38–42.

MANAGERS AND EMPLOYEES WHO ARE NOT LAWYERS (12.06)

Rule 14 (Recognised bodies – see Chapter 14) allows managers (i.e. partners in a partnership, members of an LLP or directors of companies) of recognised bodies to be solicitors, RELs, RFLS and, inter alia, non-lawyer individuals approved by the SRA under regulation 3 of the SRA Recognised Bodies Regulations 2009. The rule also permits owners (i.e. shareholders) in recognised bodies which are companies to be approved individuals but only if such individuals are also managers. The rule restricts non-lawyer participation in recognised bodies (as managers and owners) to:

- 25 per cent of the managers by number;
- 25 per cent of the shares or other ownership rights; and
- 25 per cent of the voting rights exercised or controlled.

Rule 12.06 imposes direct obligations on managers of recognised bodies and all employees of recognised sole practitioners and recognised bodies who are non-lawyers. Such individuals must not hold themselves out in any way which suggests that they are entitled to practise as a lawyer in England and Wales. Further, such individuals must not undertake specified reserved work unless under the supervision of (or in the case of advocacy in chambers, under instructions given by) a person qualified to direct such work (or where they are authorised by a regulator such as the Office of Immigration Services Commissioner).

Rules 12.03 (RFLs), 12.05 (Managers and employees authorised by another approved regulator) and 12.06 (Managers and employees who are not lawyers) contain restrictions relating to reserved work unless such work is undertaken under the supervision of (or in the case of advocacy in chambers, under instructions given by) a person qualified to direct such work. Such a person is defined in rule 24 as meaning:

> an individual who is qualified under statute to do the relevant reserved work and who is:
>
> (a) a fellow-manager; or
> (b) the employer, a manager of the firm or a fellow-employee, if the person doing the work is not a manager.

CONCLUSION

Rule 12 has been substantially amended to reflect the changes necessary for the introduction of LDPs. It requires all practice vehicles to be either recognised bodies or recognised sole practitioners and it provides details of how individuals (solicitors, RELs, RFLs, other lawyers and non-lawyers) and the recognised body itself, can practise. The rule also imposes restrictions on those who can undertake reserved work. Reserved work is defined in rule 24 as meaning the following activities:

(a) advocacy before a court or immigration tribunal;
(b) the conduct of proceedings in a court or immigration tribunal;
(c) the preparation of documents in proceedings before a court or immigration tribunal;
(d) the preparation of instruments and the lodging of documents relating to the transfer or charge of land, and the preparation of trust deeds disposing of capital, within paragraph 5 of Schedule 2 to the Legal Services Act 2007, and the preparation of any other instrument coming within sub-paragraph (1)(c) of that paragraph;
(e) the preparation of papers on which to found or oppose a grant of probate or a grant of letters of administration;
(f) the administration of oaths and statutory declarations;
(g) notarial activities within paragraph 7 of Schedule 2 to the Legal Services Act 2007.

The rule applies to all managers and employees (solicitors, other lawyers and non-lawyers) and principals must ensure that all those working within a firm are made aware of the restrictions applying to the work they undertake.

CHAPTER 13

In-house practice, etc.

INTRODUCTION

Rule 13 applies to solicitors and RELs who practise from an office in England and Wales as employees of a business which is not a recognised sole practitioner, recognised body or an authorised non-SRA firm. It sets limits upon solicitors, RELs and RFLs working in non-SRA authorised firms undertaking work outside the firm's authorisation.

The topics covered by the rule are:

- Conditions applying [to in-house practice] at all times
- Work colleagues
- Related bodies
- Pro bono work
- Associations
- Insurers
- Commercial legal advice services
- Local government
- Law centres, charities and other non-commercial advice services
- The Crown, non-departmental public bodies, and the Legal Services Commission
- Foreign law firms
- Regulatory bodies

SCOPE

In-house practice is defined in rule 24 as a solicitor's practice within 12.01(1)(e) or 12.01(2)(e) (i.e. as the employee of another person, business or organisation where a solicitor undertakes work only for his or her employer as permitted by rule 13) or within 12.02(1)(e) or 12.02(2)(e) (i.e. as the employee of another person, business or organisation where an REL undertakes work only for his or her employer as permitted by rule 13).

Rule 13 applies to solicitors and RELs practising in-house. It also provides that solicitors, RELs and RFLs in an authorised non-SRA firm must comply with the rule as if they were an in-house solicitor or REL where as a manager or employee work is undertaken outside the firm's authorisation either for the firm itself, or for work colleagues, related bodies or pro bono work.

Other than 13.04 (Pro-bono work) the rule does not apply to overseas practice. However, 15.13(2) imposes limitations on how you can practise in-house overseas. You may only act for:

(i) your employer;

(ii) a company or organisation controlled by your employer or in which your employer has a substantial measure of control;

(iii) a company in the same group as your employer;

(iv) a company which controls your employer; or

(v) an employee (including a director or a company secretary) of a company or organisation under (i) to (iv) above, provided that the matter relates to or arises out of the work of that company or organisation, does not relate to a claim arising as a result of a personal injury to the employee, and no charge is made for your work unless those costs are recoverable from another source.

However, if you are a solicitor registered in another state under the Establishment Directive with the professional body for a local legal profession you may practise in-house to the extent that a member of that legal profession is permitted to do so.

CONDITIONS APPLYING AT ALL TIMES (13.01)

Rule 12 permits you to practise as a solicitor or REL in-house provided you only undertake work for your employer or as permitted by rule 13. Rules 13.02–13.12 set out circumstances when it is permitted for an in-house solicitor or REL to act for a client other than his or her employer. Rule 13.01 sets out the common conditions applicable in these cases.

WORK COLLEAGUES (13.02)

The original rule 13.02 applied to 'fellow employees'. The 2009 Amendment Rules now apply this rule to 'work colleagues' and the rule now specifically permits solicitors, RELs and RFLs working for authorised non-SRA firms to act for their work colleagues. 'Work colleagues' are specified in rule 13.02(1) subject to the restrictions in 13.02(2). Rule 13.02(3) permits work to be undertaken for a joint owner/buyer and for a mortgagee where the work carried out for colleagues is a conveyancing transaction.

RELATED BODIES (13.03)

An in-house lawyer may act for the employer's or authorised non-SRA firm's related bodies. This includes a holding, associated or subsidiary company; a partnership, syndicate and LLP; or a company by way of a joint venture in which the employer or authorised non-SRA firm and others have an interest; a trade association of which the employer or authorised non-SRA firm is a member; or a club, association, pension fund or other scheme operated for the benefit of the employer's employees; or the employees or managers of an authorised non-SRA firm. Rule 13.03(2) disallows the provisions relating to holding, associated or subsidiary companies and partnerships, syndicates, LLPs or joint ventures where the in-house lawyer is employed in local government.

PRO BONO WORK (13.04)

Pro bono work may be conducted for a client other than an in-house lawyer's employer or authorised non-SRA firm under 13.04 and subject to conditions.

ASSOCIATIONS (13.05)

Where an in-house lawyer is employed by an association, he or she may act for a member subject to the conditions in 13.05.

INSURERS (13.06)

In-house lawyers employed by an insurer subrogated to the rights of an insured may act for the insurer in the name of the insured. Rule 13.06 also permits the lawyer to act on behalf of:

- the insured in certain other specified circumstances (including where the lawyer is employed by a legal expenses insurer);
- a defendant covered by another insurer where the insurers have agreed an apportionment of liability; and
- another insurer prosecuting a claim jointly with the employer.

COMMERCIAL LEGAL ADVICE SERVICES (13.07)

In-house solicitors or RELs employed by a commercial organisation providing a telephone legal advice service may advise enquirers by telephone only with a follow up letter when necessary. Note 24 confirms that the restrictions in 13.07 will not apply if you act for an insurer which runs a commercial legal telephone advice service and wish to act for an insured under a legal expenses insurance policy as permitted by 13.06.

LOCAL GOVERNMENT (13.08)

Rule 13.08 specifies the organisations or persons an in-house solicitor or REL employed by local government may act for. In each category, conditions are imposed by the rule. The following persons or organisations are listed in 13.08 along with the conditions applicable in each case:

- Organisations or persons to which or to whom the employer is statutorily empowered to provide legal services. For the avoidance of doubt, where these organisations or persons are specifically mentioned in 13.08, the in-house lawyer will be subject to the conditions mentioned (13.08(a)).
- Members or former members of the local authority (13.08(b)).
- Certain specified companies limited by shares or guarantee (13.08(c)).
- Lenders in connection with new mortgages arising from the redemption of mortgages to the local authority (13.08(d)).
- A charity or voluntary organisation whose objects relate wholly to the employer's area. Under 13.08(e) the in-house lawyer is permitted to act on contentious matters subject to an indemnity for costs given by the employer.
- A patient who is the subject of a Court of Protection Order (13.08(f)).
- A child or young person subject to a Care Order in favour of the employer on an application to the Criminal Injuries Compensation Authority (13.08(g)).

LAW CENTRES, CHARITIES AND OTHER NON-COMMERCIAL ADVICE SERVICES (13.09)

Rule 13.09 allows lawyers employed by law centres, etc. to give advice and otherwise act for members of the public.

Further guidance can be found in note 25.

THE CROWN, NON-DEPARTMENTAL PUBLIC BODIES, AND THE LEGAL SERVICES COMMISSION (13.10)

Rule 13.10 permits solicitors and RELs employed by the Crown, etc. to give legal advice to and to act for other persons if, in doing so, they are carrying out the lawful functions of their employers.

FOREIGN LAW FIRMS (13.11)

In-house solicitors and RELs working for foreign law firms (defined in 13.11(1)(a) and (b)) may provide legal services to their employer's clients subject to the conditions set out in 13.11(2).

Further guidance can be found in notes 26 and 27.

GUIDANCE

There is little guidance on the rule itself. New guidance has, however, been added (notes 28–30) on the position of solicitors, RELs and RFLs working for authorised non-SRA firms outside the scope of the firm's authorisation.

Additional general guidance is reasonably comprehensive. In-house lawyers will find useful guidance on the following topics:

- The need for a practising certificate (note 1). An article in the Law Society's *Gazette* by Tony Guise (see [2007] Gazette, 26 April, 16) suggests that the rule 20 obligation relating to practising certificates (see below, Chapter 20) is the opposite to that provided for in *Piper Double Glazing Limited* v. *DC Contracts (1992) Limited* [1994] 1 All ER 177. The guidance to rule 20 suggests that a practising certificate must be held where you are held out or employed explicitly or implicitly as a solicitor. Piper suggested that the requirement for a practising certificate (arising where you are 'acting as a solicitor') was limited to doing the acts which only a solicitor may perform. Tony Guise, in his article, believes the effect of the Code is to overrule *Piper* and unless an appropriate exemption applies (see rule 20 (in particular note 55) and notes 1–3 to rule 13) in-house lawyers will need a practising certificate.
- Practice outside England and Wales (note 4).
- Undertakings (note 5).
- Communications with third parties represented by another lawyer (note 6).
- Stationery and letterheads (notes 7 and 8).
- Practising address (note 9).
- Accounts and accountants' reports (notes 10–13).
- Separate practice through a firm (notes 14–18).
- Industrial action by in-house lawyers (note 19).
- Costs recovered from third parties (notes 20–22).
- Direct access to client (note 23).

CONCLUSION

Rule 13 covers the type of work that can be undertaken by in-house solicitors and RELs and solicitors, RELs and RFLs working for authorised non-SRA firms outside the scope of the firm's authorisation, rather than the general conduct obligations of such lawyers. As such a lawyer, you are bound by the conduct obligations contained in the Code in the same way as other lawyers, although on occasions the Code does make specific provision for in-house practice.

In addition to the points noted above in the guidance notes, in-house lawyers should also specifically check compliance with rules relating to:

- core duties (rule 1);
- conflicts of interest (rule 3; notes 17–22 deal with in-house practice);
- management (5.01(2) deals with in-house practice);
- supervision (5.03(2) deals with in-house practice);
- equality and diversity (6.04 deals with in-house practice);
- separate businesses (rule 21; note 7 deals with in-house practice).

The 2009 Amendment Rules have made no changes of substance to the rules as they apply to solicitors and RELs undertaking in-house practice. However, solicitors, RELs and RFLs taking advantage of the fact that they can now work for authorised non-SRA firms must understand the restrictions in rule 13 relating to work outside their firm's authorisation when acting for the firm itself, colleagues, related bodies or pro bono.

CHAPTER 14

Recognised bodies

INTRODUCTION

Rule 12 only permits solicitors and RELs to provide legal services to the public through a firm which is a recognised body or as a recognised sole practitioner.

Rule 14 sets out the requirements relating to the structure and composition of a recognised body and the services that a recognised body may provide. The requirements relating to sole practitioners are not dealt with in this rule but are covered in rule 20.01(6) and rule 20.03 – see Chapter 20 below.

Rule 14 covers the following topics:

* Fundamental requirements for all recognised bodies
* Duties in relation to compliance
* Formation, office in England and Wales and registered office
* Recognised bodies which are partnerships
* Recognised bodies which are LLPs
* Recognised bodies which are companies
* Information and documentation

In addition, reference should be made to the SRA Recognised Bodies Regulations 2009 which replaced the Solicitor's Recognised Bodies Regulations 2007 on 31 March 2009. These Regulations cover the following topics:

* **Part 1 – Applications, conditions and appeals.** Part 1 contains details of how to apply for recognised body status, the conditions that may be imposed on recognition and the appeals process. Regulation 3 contains the requirements relating to the approval of an individual who is not a lawyer of England and Wales, an REL, an RFL or an exempt European lawyer, where such individual wishes to be a manager of a recognised body.
* **Part 2 – Duration of recognition, renewal date, revocation and expiry.** Part 2 deals with the duration of recognition, including the provisions relating to passporting existing partnerships into recognised body status on 31 March 2009 and the transitional provisions. Previously recognised bodies (LLPs and companies) had recognition granted for a period of three

years. Under regulation 8 recognition is renewable yearly on 31 October. However, there are transitional provisions in 8.5, 8.6 and 8.7 applicable to bodies already recognised on 31 March 2009. If a firm's recognition commenced on or before 1 November 2006, recognition will last for three years and must be renewed at the end of that three-year period. If the firm's recognition commenced after 1 November 2006 but before 1 March 2009 the recognition will last until 31 October 2009 regardless of what is said on the certificate. Any recognition granted after 1 March 2009 but before 1 November 2009 will have to be renewed on 31 October 2009.

- **Part 3 – Name, the register and certificate of recognition.**
- **Part 4 – Interpretation, waivers, reconsideration and notifying third parties.**

SCOPE

Rule 14 applies to recognised bodies, their managers, employees and share-holders. It applies to a recognised body in relation to its overseas practice and to the overseas practice as a manager of a recognised body where the manager is a lawyer of England and Wales or an individual non-lawyer (15.14).

FUNDAMENTAL REQUIREMENTS FOR ALL RECOGNISED BODIES (14.01)

There are three fundamental requirements set out in rule 14.01:

- Services requirements
- Relevant lawyer requirements
- Management and control requirements

Rule 14.01(1) sets out the services requirements of a recognised body, restricting the business of such a body to professional services of a sort provided by individual solicitors and/or lawyers of other jurisdictions and the professional services of notaries public if the notary is acting as a manager or employee of a recognised body. However, provided the requirements of rule 21 (Separate businesses) are satisfied, rule 14 does not prevent an appropriate ownership interest in a separate business.

Rule 14.01(2) sets out the relevant lawyer requirement of a recognised body. At least one manager must be:

- a solicitor with a current practising certificate;
- an RFL; or
- in the case of a partnership or LLP, a legally qualified body where at least one manager is a solicitor with a current practising certificate or an REL. A legally qualified body is defined in rule 24 as a recognised body, an authorised non-SRA firm or a European practice of which lawyers make up at least 75 per cent of the ultimate beneficial ownership.

There are provisions dealing with situations arising which put the firm in breach (e.g. where the only or last remaining solicitor or REL is committed to prison, becomes incapable as a result of illness or abandons the practice).

Rule 14.01(3) sets out the management and control requirements. This rule requires that at least 75 per cent of the body's managers must be bodies corporate which are 'legally qualified bodies' and/or individuals who are entitled to practise as:

- lawyers of England and Wales (this covers solicitors with a practising certificate and any individual who is authorised to practise in England and Wales by an approved regulator – i.e. barristers, legal executives, licensed conveyancers, trade mark and patent agents, costs draughtsmen and notaries);
- lawyers of Establishment Directive professions;
- RFLs.

Further, at least 75 per cent of the ultimate beneficial ownership of the recognised body must belong to individuals who fall into one of the three categories noted above and such individuals must exercise or control at least 75 per cent of the voting rights of the body (and if the body is a company with shares, must hold at least 75 per cent of the shares).

Guidance note 11 provides six tests to be applied in determining the requirements of a recognised body relating to management and control.

Obviously, the rule permits up to 25 per cent of the managers, beneficial owners and/or individuals exercising voting rights to be non-lawyers. Such individuals must be approved by the SRA under regulation 3 of the SRA Recognised Bodies Regulations 2009. However, subject to a limited exception, every non-lawyer owner of a recognised body must be a manager of the body (see note 11(f)).

DUTIES IN RELATION TO COMPLIANCE (14.02)

An obligation is imposed on a recognised body to undertake certain checks before taking on a new manager. In particular, the recognised body must be satisfied as to the manager's eligibility by:

- checking that any solicitor has a practising certificate which is not subject to a condition precluding the individual from becoming a manager;
- checking that any REL or RFL is registered with the SRA and the registration is not subject to a condition precluding the individual from becoming a manager;
- obtaining and retaining for production to the SRA written confirmation from a non-SRA approved regulator that the individual is a lawyer authorised by such a regulator and checking that such authorisation is not subject to a condition precluding the individual from becoming a manager;

- obtaining and retaining for production to the SRA any non-lawyer individual's approval under regulation 3 of the SRA Recognised Bodies Regulations 2009 together with details of any event in relation to that individual which must be declared on the next renewal of recognition;
- in relation to any body corporate, checking and retaining confirmations as to the above in respect of every individual who is a manager of or who has an interest in the body corporate.

Rule 14.02 also imposes obligations on the recognised body and the managers of recognised body to ensure compliance with the rules contained in the Code and in particular rule 14.

FORMATION, OFFICE IN ENGLAND AND WALES AND REGISTERED OFFICE (14.03)

Recognised bodies which are partnerships may be formed under the law of any country and may be a legal person. However, recognised bodies which are LLPs must be incorporated in England and Wales or in Scotland under the Limited Liability Partnerships Act 2000. Further, recognised bodies which are companies must either be incorporated in England and Wales or in Scotland under the Companies Act or incorporated in an Establishment state and registered as an overseas company or incorporated and registered in an Establishment Directive state as a societas Europaea. However, in all cases the recognised body must have at least one practising address in England and Wales and must have its registered office at a practising address in England and Wales if it is registered in England and Wales.

RECOGNISED BODIES WHICH ARE PARTNERSHIPS (14.04)

Rule 14.04 sets out who may be a partner in a partnership. All or any of the following may be a partner:

- a lawyer of England and Wales (including a solicitor with a current practising certificate);
- an REL;
- an RFL;
- an exempt European lawyer;
- an individual approved by the SRA under regulation 3 of the SRA Recognised Bodies Regulations 2009;
- a body corporate which is a legally qualified body.

Where there is a change in the composition of a recognised body which is a partnership, recognition continues but the partnership must cease to practise if the change results in a breach of the fundamental requirements relating to relevant lawyers or management and control (see above 14.01). There are, however, transitional provisions which apply if the change results in only one remaining partner who needs to be recognised as a recognised sole practitioner (see 14.04(4) and (5)).

The rule also covers the situation where a partnership splits into two or more firms (14.04(6)–(9)); where circumstances occur in a partnership leading to there being only one active partner (14.04(10)); and a prohibition on a partner in a partnership creating any charge or other third party interest over his or her interest in the partnership (14.04(11)).

RECOGNISED BODIES WHICH ARE LLPS (14.05)

The rule sets out who may be a member of the LLP. All or any of the following may be a member:

- a lawyer of England and Wales (including a solicitor with a current practising certificate);
- an REL;
- an RFL;
- an exempt European lawyer;
- an individual approved by the SRA under regulation 3 of the SRA Recognised Bodies Regulations 2009;
- a body corporate which is a legally qualified body.

An LLP must have at least two members but there are transitional provisions (14.05(2)(b)) if any breach is remedied within six months. There is a prohibition on a member creating any charge or other third party interest over his or her interest in the LLP (14.05(3)).

RECOGNISED BODIES WHICH ARE COMPANIES (14.06)

The rule sets out who may be a director of a company. All or any of the following may be a director:

- a lawyer of England and Wales (including a solicitor with a current practising certificate);
- an REL;
- an RFL;
- an exempt European lawyer;
- an individual approved by the SRA under regulation 3 of the SRA Recognised Bodies Regulations 2009.

Note that directors must be individuals – there cannot be a corporate director.
Further, all or any of the following may be a member or shareowner:

- a lawyer of England and Wales (including a solicitor with a current practising certificate);
- an REL;

- an RFL;
- an exempt European lawyer;
- an individual approved by the SRA under regulation 3 of the SRA Recognised Bodies Regulations 2009;
- a legally qualified body.

A Court of Protection deputy may also be a shareholder or member in that capacity without breach of the rule, providing the person in respect of whom the deputy has been appointed remains eligible to be a member or shareowner. If the deputy is not eligible in their own right to be a member or shareholder, the deputy cannot exercise any vote in respect of the shares.

There is a prohibition on a member or shareowner creating any charge or other third party interest over his or her interest in the company, except by way of holding a share as nominee for a non-member shareowner who is eligible to be a shareowner as above. In such a case, the recognised body must keep a record of any non-member shareowners and retain the record for at least three years after their ownership ceases.

Rule 14.06 also contains obligations relating to:

- the death of a member or shareowner (14.06(5));
- a member or shareowner ceasing to be eligible (14.06(6));
- a member or shareowner becoming insolvent but not ineligible (14.06(7)).

INFORMATION AND DOCUMENTATION (14.07)

Rule 14.07 sets out the requirements relating to the notification and supply of certain specified information to the SRA.

OTHER GUIDANCE

Notes 13–21 provide guidance on some regulatory provisions; note 22 provides guidance on compliance with other rules, e.g. the Solicitors' Indemnity Insurance Rules, the Solicitors' Accounts Rules, the Solicitors' Financial Services (Scope) Rules and the Solicitors' Financial Services (Conduct of Business) Rules; note 26 covers the steps to be taken in order to deal with certain emergencies; and notes 27–30 provide guidance on executor, trustee and nominee companies, secretarial companies, and service companies.

CONCLUSION

Rule 14 has been substantially amended as a result of the 2009 Amendment Rules. However, for existing firms of solicitors wishing to continue practising in the same mode as they were prior to 31 March 2009 there should be no need for any action to be taken immediately. Existing partnerships will have been passported into recognition on 31 March 2009. Existing LLPs and companies should already have obtained recognised body status.

However, there are some points to bear in mind for the future:

- Recognition will expire on 31 October 2009 and must be renewed on that date (regardless of whether your existing recognition was originally granted for a longer period).
- All new firms (partnerships, LLPs or companies) must seek and obtain recognition before commencing practice.
- Where new managers are to be appointed the body must check eligibility and retain appropriate documentation for production to the SRA.

CHAPTER 15

Overseas practice

INTRODUCTION

Rule 15 applies to overseas practice, which is defined in rule 24 as:

(a) the practice from an office outside England and Wales of:

    (i) a solicitor;

    (ii) a recognised body;

    (iii) a manager of a recognised body who is a lawyer of England and Wales;

(b) the activities of an individual non-lawyer as a manager of a recognised body practising from an office outside England and Wales;

(c) the activities of a body corporate as a manager of a recognised body practising from an office outside England and Wales; and

(d) the practice of an REL from an office or offices in Scotland or Northern Ireland;

    ...

The definition has been amended by the 2009 Amendment Rules to reflect the changes introduced by the Legal Services Act 2007 so that the overseas activities of managers who are not solicitors are brought within the definition.

The Code applies to practice both within England and Wales and overseas, with adjustments made (either by way of disapplying rules or by substituting different rules) for overseas practice. Rule 15 provides the detail.

There is specific provision made in rule 15 for accounts, deposit interest and professional indemnity because the equivalent domestic rules (the Solicitors' Accounts Rules 1998 and the Solicitors' Indemnity Insurance Rules) do not apply overseas.

Rule 15 deals with the following topics:

- Core duties (rule 1) application, and conflicts of rules (15.01)
- Overseas requirements relating to rules 2–14 (15.02–15.14)
- Deposit interest (15.15)
- Overseas requirements relating to rules 16–25 (15.16–15.25)
- Professional indemnity (15.26)
- Accounts (15.27)

SCOPE (15.01)

Application to overseas practice (15.01(2))

Rule 15.01(2)(a) applies rule 15 in relation to practice from an office outside the UK to:

- a solicitor as an individual, whether or not the solicitor's firm or employer is subject to these rules;
- a solicitor-controlled recognised body (defined in rule 24 as a recognised body in which lawyers of England and Wales constitute the national group of lawyers with the largest (or equal largest) share of control of the recognised body); and
- a lawyer of England and Wales other than a solicitor and a non-lawyer, in relation to practice as a manager of a solicitor-controlled recognised body.

Rule 15.01(2)(b) covers the position in relation to practice from an office in Scotland or Northern Ireland. While solicitors as individuals, solicitor-controlled recognised bodies and non-solicitor managers will be subject to rule 15 when practising in Scotland or Northern Ireland, RELs will also be subject to rule 15 in respect of such practice (whether practising as individuals or through an REL-controlled recognised body).

In both cases the rule makes it clear that solicitor and REL managers and employees will be subject to the obligations in rule 15 (where applicable) notwithstanding the fact that the recognised body is not so subject because it is not a solicitor-controlled recognised body or (in Scotland or Northern Ireland) it is not an REL-controlled recognised body.

One consequence of the application of rule 15 is that the rule does not apply to RELs as individuals practising in an office outside the UK – it only applies to RELs as individuals practising from an office in Scotland or Northern Ireland. Further, unlike other rules in the Code, rule 15 does not apply to non-lawyer employees of a recognised body or a recognised sole practitioner, nor does it apply to RFLs in respect of overseas practice.

Application to overseas activities outside the scope of practice (15.01(1)(b))

Solicitors, RELs and RFLs are subject to certain specified rules in relation to activities undertaken outside England and Wales which fall outside the scope of practice, whether these activities are undertaken as a lawyer or in some other business or private capacity. The applicable rules are as follows (15.01(1)(b)):

- 1.06 (Public confidence – see Chapter 1 above) will apply to solicitors, RELs and RFLs;
- 10.01 (Not taking unfair advantage – see Chapter 10 above) will apply to solicitors and, within the UK only, to the behaviour of RELs;

- 15.10(2)(a)(ii) and (iii), (b) and (c) (undertakings given outside the scope of practice) will apply to solicitors and, within the UK only, to RELs;
- 12.03(2) and (3) (practice in another capacity than an RFL) and 12.03(4)(a) (holding out as a lawyer of England and Wales) will apply to RFLs;
- 12.03(5) (wrongly doing immigration work) will apply to an RFL's activities in Scotland or Northern Ireland.

Compliance with local law (15.01(4))

If compliance with any of the rules applicable to overseas practice would result in a breach of local law, the appropriate provision may be disregarded to the extent that it is necessary for compliance with the local law.

CORE DUTIES (RULE 1) (15.01)

Rule 1 (Core duties) applies to overseas practice.

OVERSEAS REQUIREMENTS RELATING TO RULES 2–14 (15.02–15.14)

The provisions of 15.02–15.14 are dealt with in the appropriate chapters above (Chapters 2–14) covering the scope of rules 2–14.

DEPOSIT INTEREST (15.15)

Rule 15.15 applies where client money is held overseas. Client money is defined in rule 24 as meaning money 'you receive or hold for or on behalf of a client or trust'. (This definition is narrower than the definition of client money in the Solicitors' Accounts Rules 1998. The Solicitors' Accounts Rules only apply to domestic practice.) The provisions of 15.15 must be complied with if you are:

- a solicitor sole practitioner practising from an office outside England and Wales or an REL sole practitioner practising from an office in Scotland or Northern Ireland;
- a solicitor-controlled recognised body or, in relation to practice in Scotland or Northern Ireland, an REL-controlled recognised body;
- a solicitor manager of a firm which is practising from an office outside the UK and solicitors control the firm;
- a solicitor or REL manager of a firm which is practising from an office in Scotland or Northern Ireland and solicitors and/or RELs control the firm.

Where 15.15 applies, it requires interest to be paid to a client where, in fairness, the client money held for the client ought to have earned interest for the client.

OVERSEAS REQUIREMENTS RELATING TO RULES 16–25 (15.16–15.25)

The provisions of 15.16–15.25 are dealt with in the appropriate chapters below (Chapters 16–25) covering the scope of rules 16–25.

PROFESSIONAL INDEMNITY (15.26)

Rule 15.26 requires that in relation to overseas practice you are covered by insurance or other indemnity against professional liabilities. The amount of cover need not exceed the equivalent amount required for domestic practice but must be reasonable having regard to the matters expressed in 15.26(2)(b).

ACCOUNTS (15.27)

The provisions in 15.27 apply to client money (defined as above). Rule 15.27 must be complied with where you receive client money in relation to practice from an office outside the UK if you are (15.27(1)):

(a) a solicitor sole practitioner who has held or received client money;
(b) a solicitor-controlled recognised body which has held or received client money as a firm;
(c) a lawyer of England and Wales, or a non-lawyer, who is a manager of a solicitor-controlled recognised body which holds or receives client money;
(d) a solicitor manager of any other firm which is controlled by solicitors, either directly as partners, members or owners, or indirectly by their ownership of bodies corporate which are partners, members or owners, if the firm holds or receives client money;
(e) a solicitor who holds or receives client money as a named trustee;
(f) a lawyer of England and Wales, or a non-lawyer, who is a manager of a solicitor-controlled recognised body and who holds or receives client money as a named trustee.

Rule 15.27(2) covers the position in relation to practice from an office in Scotland or Northern Ireland and applies the rule to such practice undertaken by those noted in 15.27(1) but also to RELs and REL-controlled recognised bodies.

Where rule 27 applies, dealings with client money must be undertaken in accordance with 15.27(3).

Rule 15.27(4) deals with accountants' reports.

Notes 26–28 provide some additional guidance on the accounts rules as applicable to overseas practice.

CONCLUSION

In addition to the obligations under rule 15, an overseas practice will be subject to many of the other rules in the Code. Below is a checklist identifying which specific rules will apply to overseas practice (details can be found in the appropriate chapters of this Companion).

- Rule 1 (Core duties): applicable in full.
- Rule 2 (Client relations): not applicable but see 15.02(2)–(4).
- Rule 3 (Conflict of interests): applicable except 3.07–3.22 if the property is overseas.
- Rule 4 (Confidentiality and disclosure): applicable in full.
- Rule 5 (Business management in England and Wales): not applicable but see 15.05(2) and (4).
- Rule 6 (Equality and diversity): not applicable.
- Rule 7 (Publicity): applicable except to electronic communications from an office in the EU and 7.07 (Letterhead, website and e-mails) subject to the requirements of 15.07(3)(a) and (b).
- Rule 8 (Fee sharing): applicable except 8.02 (Fee sharing with other non-lawyers) does not apply to European cross-border practice.
- Rule 9 (Referrals of business): not applicable.
- Rule 10 (Relations with third parties): applicable except 10.05 (Undertakings, but see 15.10(2)) and 10.06 (if land is situated outside England and Wales).
- Rule 11 (Litigation and advocacy): only applicable if the court, tribunal, etc. is in England and Wales.
- Rule 12 (Framework of practice): applicable.
- Rule 13 (In-house practice): not applicable except 13.04 (Pro bono work). However, see 15.13(2).
- Rule 14 (Recognised bodies): applicable subject to the provisions of 15.14(2) and (3).
- Rule 15 (Overseas practice): applicable.
- Rule 16 (European cross-border practice): applicable where overseas practice is involved in European cross-border activities.
- Rule 17 (Insolvency practice): only applicable to appointments appertaining to orders made in England and Wales.
- Rule 18 (Property selling): only applicable to a practice from an office in Scotland or Northern Ireland.
- Rule 19 (Financial services): only applicable to regulated activities conducted from an office in Scotland or Northern Ireland or to regulated activities conducted into the UK from an overseas office.
- Rule 20 (Rights and obligations of practice): applicable.
- Rule 21 (Separate businesses): rule 21 applies where you practise from an office in England and Wales and the separate business is overseas. However rule 21 does not apply where you practise from an office outside England and Wales and you have a separate business (15.21(1)(b)). In these circumstances see 15.21(2).
- Rule 22 (Waivers): applicable.

- Rule 23 (Application of these rules): only rule 23.01(3) applies, which provides that the rules apply to practice from an office outside England and Wales to the extent specified in rule 15.
- Rules 24 (Interpretation) and 25 (Commencement and repeals): applicable in full.

CHAPTER 16

European cross-border practice

INTRODUCTION

Rule 16 applies to European cross-border activities. These are defined in 16.01(1) as:

(i) any professional activity in a CCBE state other than the UK, whether or not you are physically present in that CCBE state; and

(ii) any professional contact with a lawyer of a CCBE state other than the UK.

(CCBE is the Council of the Bars and Law Societies of Europe.) For the purposes of this rule, professional contacts and professional activities taking place within a firm or in-house legal department are not European cross-border practice.

Note 1 lists the CCBE states and their legal professions for the purposes of defining cross-border activities.

Before 1 July 2007, those involved in cross-border activities had to comply with the Law Society's (or the SRA's) rules of conduct together with the provisions of the CCBE Code of Conduct for European Lawyers. The CCBE Code contains a large number of obligations. Most of these obligations are replicated in other parts of the Solicitors' Code of Conduct 2007 – rule 16 simply contains those obligations from the CCBE Code that are not contained elsewhere in the Code of Conduct.

Consequently, compliance with rule 16 and the rest of the Code will ensure compliance with the CCBE Code.

Rule 16 deals with the following topics:

- Occupations considered incompatible with legal practice
- Fee sharing with non-lawyers
- Co-operation between lawyers of different CCBE states
- Correspondence between lawyers in different CCBE states
- Paying referral fees to non-lawyers
- Disputes between lawyers in different member states

SCOPE

Rule 16.01(2) specifies that the rule will apply as follows:

(a) If you are a solicitor this rule applies to your European cross-border practice from an office in, or outside, England and Wales.

(b) If you are an REL this rule applies to your European cross-border practice from an office within the UK.

(c) If you are an RFL and you are a manager or employee of a recognised body or the employee of a recognised sole practitioner, this rule applies to your European cross-border practice from an office in England and Wales.

(d) This rule applies to a recognised body as follows:

  (i) A solicitor-controlled recognised body is subject to the rule in relation to its European cross-border practice from any of its offices, wherever situated.

  (ii) An REL-controlled recognised body is subject to the rule in relation to its European cross-border practice from any of its offices in the UK.

  (iii) A recognised body which is not within (i) or (ii) is subject to the rule in relation to its European cross-border practice from any of its offices in England and Wales.

(e) If you are a manager of a recognised body and you are not a solicitor but you are a lawyer of England and Wales or a non-lawyer, this rule applies to you to the extent that the rule applies to the body itself under (d) above.

(f) If you are a manager of a recognised body and you are registered with the Bar Standards Board under the Establishment Directive, this rule applies to your European cross-border practice from an office of the recognised body in the UK to the extent that the rule applies to the body itself under (d) above.

The rule applies to overseas practice to the extent that such practice is European cross-border practice (15.16).

OCCUPATIONS CONSIDERED INCOMPATIBLE WITH LEGAL PRACTICE (16.02)

In legal proceedings in a CCBE state other than the UK you must comply with any rules, as they apply to local lawyers, regarding occupations incompatible with the practice of law. Where you are based in an office in a CCBE state you must respect any rules regarding participation in commercial or other activities not connected with the practice of law applicable to local lawyers. Notes 3 and 4 provide additional guidance on 16.02. This rule repeats the provisions of the CCBE Code, article 2.5.

FEE SHARING WITH NON-LAWYERS (16.03)

You must not share your professional fees with a non-lawyer situated in a CCBE state other than the UK except as permitted by 16.03(1). If you practise from an office in a CCBE state other than the UK, whether or not you are physically present at the office, you must not share your professional fees from that office with a non-lawyer except as permitted by 16.03(2). In both cases fee sharing is permitted within a firm if such fee sharing is allowed by rule 12 (Framework of practice) – see Chapter 12 above. Notes 5–7 provide further guidance on 16.03. This rule repeats the provisions of the CCBE Code, article 3.

CO-OPERATION BETWEEN LAWYERS OF DIFFERENT CCBE STATES (16.04)

You are required to assist lawyers of a CCBE state other than the UK to obtain information necessary to find and instruct a lawyer competent to undertake specific services where you are not competent to provide those services. This rule repeats the provisions of the CCBE Code, article 5.

CORRESPONDENCE BETWEEN LAWYERS IN DIFFERENT CCBE STATES (16.05)

Rule 16.05(1) covers the position where you are corresponding with a lawyer of a CCBE state other than the UK and you wish the correspondence to remain confidential or without prejudice. Before sending such correspondence you must express your intention clearly and ask if the lawyer is able to accept the correspondence on this basis. If you receive correspondence from another CCBE state which is stated to be confidential or without prejudice and you are unable to accept it on that basis, you must follow the requirements of 16.05(2). Further guidance is provided in notes 8–10. This rule repeats the provisions of the CCBE Code, article 5.3.

PAYING REFERRAL FEES TO NON-LAWYERS (16.06)

You must not pay a fee, commission or any other compensation for referring a client:

(a) if the non-lawyer is situated in a CCBE state other than the UK; or
(b) if you are practising from an office in a CCBE state other than the UK, whether or not you are physically present at that office.

This rule repeats the provisions of the CCBE Code, article 5.4, and further guidance can be found in notes 11–13.

DISPUTES BETWEEN LAWYERS IN DIFFERENT MEMBER STATES (16.07)

The procedure to follow in the event of a dispute with a lawyer of a CCBE state other than the UK is specified in 16.07. Note 14 provides further guidance. This rule repeats the provisions of the CCBE Code, article 5.9.

CONCLUSION

Other than the change in the scope of this rule, the 2009 Amendment Rules make no changes of substance to this rule.

CHAPTER 17

Insolvency practice

SCOPE

The rule applies to solicitors and RELs who are insolvency practitioners in a firm. The rule does not apply to overseas practice except in relation to appointments appertaining to orders made in the courts of England and Wales (15.17).

Rule 17 does not apply to solicitors, RELs or RFLs practising through or employed by an authorised non-SRA firm when doing work of a sort authorised by the firm's approved regulators.

INSOLVENCY PRACTICE (17.01)

The provisions of 17.01 apply when you accept an appointment or act as an appointment holder as an insolvency practitioner. You must comply with the Code of Ethics produced by the Joint Insolvency Committee and adopted by the Solicitors Regulation Authority Board.

Guidance notes 1 and 2 remind insolvency practitioners that they must also comply with the requirements of any relevant legislation and that they should also have regard to other guidance and best practice promulgated from time to time by the SRA as a recognised professional body.

CHAPTER 18

Property selling

INTRODUCTION

Rule 18 deals with property selling through your firm. Rule 21 deals with property selling through a separate business.

The rule stresses that when you undertake property selling services, the seller is your client and the contents of this rule add to the same law and professional rules binding upon you in relation to your other work.

The rule covers the following topics:

- Standards of property selling services
- Statement on the cost
- Conflict of interests
- Waivers

SCOPE

Rule 18 applies (in relation to property selling services only) to:

- solicitors or RELs practising from offices in England and Wales (including recognised sole practitioners practising as solicitors or RELs);
- recognised bodies (all practices other than recognised sole practitioners must now be recognised bodies);
- any other person who is a manager or employee of a recognised body or the employee of a recognised sole practitioner practising from offices in England and Wales;
- any RFL practising from offices in England and Wales as an employee of a recognised sole practitioner; a manager, employee, owner or director of a recognised body; or as a manager, member or owner of a body corporate which is a manager, member or owner of a recognised body.

Rule 18 applies to practice from an office in Scotland or Northern Ireland but not to practice from an office outside the UK.

Rule 18 does not apply to solicitors, RELs or RFLs practising through or employed by an authorised non-SRA firm when doing work of a sort authorised by the firm's approved regulators.

STANDARDS OF PROPERTY SELLING SERVICES (18.01)

When providing property selling services through your firm you must comply with the standards listed in 18.01(1):

- You must ensure the service is provided with sufficient competence.
- You must not seek from any prospective buyer a pre-contract deposit in excess of any prescribed limit.
- You must promptly send to your client written accurate details of any offer you have received from a prospective buyer in respect of an interest in the property (other than those of a description which your client has indicated in writing that they do not want to receive).

A new rule was introduced in 2007 (18.01(2)) which provides:

> If you are the person who is responsible for marketing a residential property you must comply with any Home Information Packs Regulations made under the Housing Act 2004.

New guidance on compliance with HIPs was also issued in August 2007. This now appears in note 11(g). Notes 10 and 11 provide guidance on the Estate Agents Act 1979. The exemption from that Act for practising solicitors is based on the fact that standards required by the Act already apply to solicitors. These standards are those contained in rule 18 and other applicable rules in the Code.

STATEMENT ON THE COST (18.02)

Certain information must be given to the client in a written statement at the outset and before the client is committed to any liability towards you.

Rule 18.02 corresponds with the requirements under the Estate Agents Act 1979.

Notes 12–18 provide additional guidance on these requirements.

CONFLICT OF INTERESTS (18.03)

As well as the requirements of rule 3 (see above Chapter 3), when selling property the additional requirements set out in 18.03 must be followed. Again, these requirements correspond with the equivalent obligations under the Estate Agents Act 1979.

This rule applies also to anyone with whom you carry on a joint property selling practice and owners of an associated firm.

WAIVERS (18.04)

Because rule 18 sets the standards equivalent to those set under the Estate Agents Act 1979, the Board of the SRA has no power to waive any of the provisions of this rule.

OTHER GUIDANCE

Rule 18 is limited to the equivalent standards under the Estate Agents Act 1979. However some of good practice guidance is contained in notes 1–9. These notes contain guidance on:

- selling property through a separate business (notes 1, 8 and 9);
- SEALs as defined in 3.12 (note 2);
- Property Display Centres. Notes 3, 4 and 5 define such centres and provide details of the limitations applicable;
- sharing fees with sub-agents (note 6);
- structural surveys (note 7).

CONCLUSION

Since rule 18 incorporates the standards required by the Estate Agents Act 1979, there is no change of substance as a result of the 2009 Amendment Rules other than the general changes relating to scope.

CHAPTER 19

Financial services

INTRODUCTION

Rule 19 sets out the requirements in connection with the provision of financial services.

SCOPE

Rule 19 applies to:

- solicitors or RELs practising from offices in England and Wales (including recognised sole practitioners practising as solicitors or RELs);
- recognised bodies (all practices other than recognised sole practitioners must now be recognised bodies);
- any other person who is a manager or employee of a recognised body or the employee of a recognised sole practitioner practising from offices in England and Wales;
- any RFL practising from offices in England and Wales as an employee of a recognised sole practitioner; a manager, employee, owner or director of a recognised body; or as a manager, member or owner of a body corporate which is a manager, member or owner of a recognised body.

The rule applies to regulated activities conducted from an office in Scotland and Northern Ireland and it also applies to regulated activities conducted into the UK from an office overseas.

Rule 19 does not apply to solicitors, RELs or RFLs practising through or employed by an authorised non-SRA firm when doing work of a sort authorised by the firm's approved regulators.

INDEPENDENCE (19.01)

Rule 19 applies to any activities in connection with any regulated activity (specified in the Financial Services and Markets Act 2000 (Regulated Activities) Order 2001, SI 2001/544) and prohibits you:

- from being an appointed representative or from having active involvement in certain separate businesses which are appointed representatives; and
- from having arrangements under which you could be constrained to recommend to clients (or refrain from doing so) certain specified transactions.

The restrictions relating to arrangements do not apply to certain specified investments. Notes 1–7 provide limited guidance on the legislation, the Solicitors' Financial Services (Scope) Rules 2001 and the Solicitors' Financial Services (Conduct of Business) Rules 2001.

CONCLUSION

There are no changes of substance to rule 19 as a result of the 2009 Amendment Rules other than the general changes relating to scope.

CHAPTER 20

Rights and obligations of practice

INTRODUCTION

Rule 20 brings together a number of statutory requirements (e.g. practising certificates, reserved work) and responsibilities owed to the SRA as the profession's regulator.

The rule covers the following topics:

- Reserved work and immigration work
- Practising certificates
- Sole practitioners
- Participation in legal practice
- Duty to co-operate with the Solicitors Regulation Authority and the Legal Complaints Service
- Reporting serious misconduct and serious financial difficulty
- Obstructing complaints
- Production of documents, information and explanations
- Dealing with claims
- Compliance with conditions

SCOPE

Rule 20 applies to:

- solicitors or RELs practising from offices in England and Wales (including recognised sole practitioners practising as solicitors or RELs);
- recognised bodies (all practices other than recognised sole practitioners must now be recognised bodies);
- any other person who is a manager or employee of a recognised body or the employee of a recognised sole practitioner practising from offices in England and Wales;
- any RFL practising from offices in England and Wales as an employee of a recognised sole practitioner; a manager, employee, owner or director of a recognised body; or as a manager, member or owner of a body corporate which is a manager, member or owner of a recognised body.

The rule applies fully to overseas practice (15.20). The rule also applies to solicitors, RELs and RFLs practising through or employed by a non-SRA authorised firm when undertaking work of the sort authorised by the firm's approved regulator.

RESERVED WORK AND IMMIGRATION WORK (20.01)

Rule 20.01 authorises individuals and recognised bodies to undertake specified reserved work and immigration work. Reserved work is defined in the Legal Services Act 2007, Sched.2 as a 'reserved legal activity'. Immigration work (which covers immigration advice and services) is restricted to certain persons by the Immigration and Asylum Act 1999. When such work involves the courts or immigration tribunals, it will be reserved work. Other immigration work, while not reserved, must only be undertaken by those authorised to do it. The rule specifies what type of reserved work and immigration work can be undertaken by:

- solicitors;
- RELs;
- RFLs;
- recognised bodies;
- recognised sole practitioners.

Certain types of reserved work can be undertaken by an unqualified person under the supervision of a manager or fellow employee suitably qualified to do that work. See the Legal Services Act 2007, Sched.3.

Guidance can be found in notes 2–9.

PRACTISING CERTIFICATES (20.02)

Solicitors practising as solicitors must hold a practising certificate whether practising in a firm or in-house, unless exempt from doing so (20.02(1)); 'practising as a solicitor' is defined in 20.02(2) for these purposes.

This rule has been amended to include the words 'whether practising in a firm or in-house'. However, note 55 sets out the specific circumstances where in-house solicitors are required to hold a practising certificate. Such solicitors will not be required to hold a practising certificate unless:

(a) they are held out or employed explicitly as a solicitor, or held out or employed implicitly as a solicitor by using a description or title such as 'lawyer' or 'counsel';
(b) they do reserved work (other than at the direction and under the supervision of a fellow employee as provided in the Solicitors Act 1974 or under the Legal Services Act 2007, Sched.3);
(c) they rely on their qualification as a solicitor in order to instruct counsel;

(d) they fulfil the role of a 'person qualified to supervise' in the limited circumstances set out in 5.02(1)(c) (law centres), (d)(i) (legal aid) or (d)(ii) (litigation or advocacy for members of the public); or

(e) they authorise the withdrawal of money from a client account, under rule 23(1)(a) of the Solicitors' Accounts Rules 1998.

Comprehensive guidance is provided in notes 10–21, including guidance on the Solicitors Act 1974, s.1 and s.88 (exemptions).

SOLE PRACTITIONERS (20.03)

Rule 20.03 requires sole practitioners to be first authorised by the SRA as a recognised sole practitioner before practising as such unless they are exempt from the obligation to be a recognised sole practitioner.

Rule 20.03(2) lists the circumstances when an exemption will apply. As a sole practitioner you will not need to be recognised in the following circumstances:

(a) your practice is conducted entirely from an office or offices outside England and Wales;

(b) your practice consists entirely of work as a temporary or permanent employee and any firm which employs you takes full responsibility for you as an employee; or

(c) your practice consists entirely of:

(i) providing professional services without remuneration for friends, relatives, companies wholly owned by you or your family, or registered charities;

(ii) administering oaths and statutory declarations; and/or

(iii) activities which could constitute practice but are done in the course of discharging the functions of any of the offices or appointments listed in paragraph (b) of the definition of 'Private Practice' in rule 3.1 of the Solicitors' Indemnity Insurance Rules.

Rule 20.03(3) covers the position when a recognised sole practitioner dies.

Notes 22–25 provide guidance on the requirements relating to sole practitioners.

PARTICIPATION IN LEGAL PRACTICE (20.04)

Solicitors, RELs and RFLs who are managers, members or owners of recognised bodies or who are employed in England and Wales in connection with the provision of legal services by a recognised body, recognised sole practitioner or an authorised non-SRA firm must do so as a solicitor, REL or RFL. Consequently such individuals, even if they are able to participate in some other capacity, cannot avoid the obligations of rule 20 and the other rules contained in the Code.

DUTY TO CO-OPERATE WITH THE SOLICITORS REGULATION AUTHORITY AND THE LEGAL COMPLAINTS SERVICE (20.05)

Dealings with the SRA and the Legal Complaints Service (LCS) must be open, prompt and co-operative. Rule 20.05(2) states that you must:

(a) provide the Solicitors Regulation Authority with information necessary in order to issue you with a practising certificate, or deal with renewal of registration or renewal of recognition, as appropriate; and

(b) during the period your practising certificate, registration or recognition is in force, notify the Authority of any changes to relevant information about you or your firm or in-house practice.

An additional obligation has been added by the 2009 Amendment Rules (20.05(3)). Where required by the SRA, as a solicitor, REL, RFL or recognised body you must act promptly to:

(a) investigate whether any person may have a claim for redress resulting from an act or omission of yours;

(b) provide the Solicitors Regulation Authority with a report on the outcome of such an investigation, identifying persons who may have such a claim;

(c) notify such persons that they may have a right of redress against you, providing them with information as to the nature of the possible claim, about the firm's complaints procedures and about the Legal Complaints Service;

(d) where you have identified a person who may have a claim for redress, ensure that the matter is dealt with under the firm's complaints procedures as if that person had made a complaint.

Guidance on 20.05 can be found in notes 27–32.

REPORTING SERIOUS MISCONDUCT AND SERIOUS FINANCIAL DIFFICULTY (20.06)

Rule 20.06 requires a report to the SRA if:

(a) you become aware of serious misconduct by a solicitor, an REL, an RFL, a recognised body, a manager of a recognised body, or an employee of a recognised body or recognised sole practitioner;

(b) you have reason to doubt the integrity of a solicitor, an REL or an RFL, a manager of a recognised body or an employee of a recognised body or recognised sole practitioner; or

(c) you have reason to believe that a solicitor, an REL, an RFL, a recognised body, a manager of a recognised body, or a firm is in serious financial difficulty which could put the public at risk.

This part of the rule has been extended to include a requirement to report on recognised bodies and employees.

Notes 33–39 provide further guidance on this requirement.

OBSTRUCTING COMPLAINTS (20.07)

The provisions of 20.07 oblige you not to hinder or prevent a person who wishes to report your conduct to the SRA or LCS. It also prohibits you from victimising a person who has made such a report. No agreement can be entered into precluding the SRA or LCS from investigating any professional misconduct and you must not issue defamation proceedings in respect of a complaint made to the SRA or LCS unless you can properly allege malice.

Notes 40 and 41 provide additional guidance. There is no change of substance.

PRODUCTION OF DOCUMENTS, INFORMATION AND EXPLANATIONS (20.08)

You must promptly comply with a written notice from the SRA that you must disclose for inspection by the appointee of the SRA all documents held by you or held under your control and all information and explanations requested (20.08(1)(a)):

(i) in connection with your practice; or

(ii) in connection with any trust of which you are, or formerly were, a trustee;

for the purpose of ascertaining whether any person subject to these rules is complying with or has complied with any provision of these or any other rules, codes or mandatory guidance made or issued by the Solicitors Regulation Authority ...

There is also a requirement to comply with notice issued by the SRA under the Solicitors Act 1974, ss.44B or 44BA.

A new 20.08(4) has been added detailing how a notice under this rule is deemed to be served.

Notes 42–44 provide additional guidance.

DEALING WITH CLAIMS (20.09)

Rule 20.09 requires clients to be notified when you become aware of acts or omissions that could give rise to a claim. Further, in these circumstances or where the client makes a claim or notifies an intention to do so you must:

(a) inform the client that independent advice should be sought (unless the client's loss, if any, is trivial and you promptly remedy that loss);

(b) consider whether a conflict of interests has arisen, and if so not act further for the client in the matter giving rise to the claim; and

(c) notify your compulsory professional indemnity insurer under the Solicitors' Indemnity Insurance Rules or 15.26 or, if appropriate, the Solicitors Indemnity Fund Ltd.

Further guidance can be found in notes 45–53.

COMPLIANCE WITH CONDITIONS (20.10)

Rule 20.10 is new and requires solicitors, RELs, RFLs and recognised bodies to comply with any condition imposed by the SRA on a practising certificate, registration or recognition.

CONCLUSION

The requirements of rule 20 have not changed significantly as a result of the 2009 Amendment Rules except in relation to the requirement for sole practitioners to be recognised. Additional notes have been added regarding the requirement for in-house lawyers to hold practising certificates and, as with other rules, changes have been made as a result of the Legal Services Act 2007, including the extension of obligations to employees.

CHAPTER 21

Separate businesses

INTRODUCTION

Rule 21 deals with the provision of services outside the practice of a solicitor, REL or RFL. 'Separate business' is defined in rule 24 as:

> a business which is not a recognised body, a recognised sole practitioner, an authorised non-SRA firm or a firm within 12.01(2)(a)–(d) or 12.02(2)(a)–(d) but which offers a service or services that could properly be offered by a recognised body ...

The introduction to the rule provides commentary upon the purpose behind the rule. The guidance on the definition of a 'separate business' was amended in July 2007 by adding some examples of the type of services which could be properly offered by a firm or in-house practice. These examples currently appear as part of note 1 to rule 21 as follows:

> ... for instance, title checks, searches, etc. for the provision of Home Information Packs.

The topics covered by the rule are:

- General [obligations]
- Services which may not be provided through a separate business
- Services which may be provided in conjunction with a firm or in-house practice
- Services which may be provided (subject to these rules) either through a firm or in-house practice, or through a separate business
- Safeguards in relation to a separate business

SCOPE

The scope of this rule is outlined in 21.01:

(1) If you are practising from an office in England and Wales as a solicitor, REL, RFL or recognised body, or if you are a manager or employee of a recognised

body, or an employee of a recognised sole practitioner, you must comply with the provisions of this rule in relation to:

   (a) services which may not be provided through a separate business;

   (b) services which may be provided through a separate business or (subject to these rules) through a firm or in-house practice; and

   (c) services which fall outside the scope of a solicitor's practice but which may be provided in conjunction with a firm or in-house practice.

(2) This rule applies to your involvement in any separate business whether the separate business is in England and Wales or outside the jurisdiction.

(3) For the avoidance of doubt, in this rule 'practising' includes practising as an in-house solicitor or an in-house REL.

Rule 21 applies where the separate business is in England and Wales or overseas. However, rule 21 does not apply where you practise from an office outside England and Wales and you have a separate business (15.21). In these circumstances, 15.21(2) imposes a number of requirements:

- There must be no contravention of rule 1 (Core duties) (15.21(2)(a)).
- The separate business must not be held out in a way suggesting that it is carrying on a practice of a lawyer regulated by the SRA (15.21(2)(b)).
- All paperwork, etc. of the separate business must be kept separate from that of any firm or in-house practice (15.21(2)(c)).
- The firm's or in-house practice's client account must not be used to hold money for the separate business (15.21(2)(d)).
- Specific information must be provided to the client where the firm or in-house practice refers a client to the separate business (15.21(2)(e)).

In-house lawyers providing services to their employer in accordance with rule 13 are not providing services through a separate business. However, note 7 confirms that rule 21 (or rule 15.21 where the employment is overseas) will apply where in-house lawyers have a separate business in addition to their in-house practice.

    Rule 21 does apply to solicitors, RELs and RFLs practising through or employed by an authorised non-SRA firm when doing work of a sort authorised by the firm's approved regulator

SERVICES WHICH MAY NOT BE PROVIDED THROUGH A SEPARATE BUSINESS (21.02)

The services that may not be provided through a separate business (subject to 21.02(2)) are listed in 21.02(1). These are:

   (a) the conduct of any matter which could come before a court, tribunal or inquiry, whether or not proceedings are started;

   (b) advocacy before a court, tribunal or inquiry;

   (c) instructing counsel in any part of the UK;

   (d) immigration advice or immigration services;

(e) any activity in relation to conveyancing, applications for probate or letters of administration, or drawing trust deeds or court documents, which is reserved to solicitors and others under the Solicitors Act 1974;

(f) drafting wills;

(g) acting as nominee, trustee or executor in England and Wales;

(h) legal advice not included above; or

(i) drafting legal documents not included above.

There are a number of exceptions to 21.02(1) listed in 21.02(2). The exceptions do not allow you to provide any reserved work through a separate business (reserved litigation, advocacy, conveyancing and probate services or immigration services) but they do allow you to undertake some of the prohibited activities in 21.02(1) as a separate business.

They are:

- practice as a lawyer of another jurisdiction;
- acting as a parliamentary agent;
- services through a separate business which is a wholly owned nominee company operated as a subsidiary but necessary part of a separate business providing financial services;
- the provision of certain legal advice and/or legal drafting as a subsidiary but necessary part of some other main service of a permitted separate business;

Notes 8–12 provide additional guidance.

The 2009 Amendment Rules have removed two categories of separate businesses from this list of exceptions:

- trade mark agents, patent agents and European patent attorneys; and
- a separate business which is an overseas separate business and which has no office in England and Wales; does not receive customers from direct or indirect referral from the practice; does not provide any services relating to the UK; and does not provide executor, trustee or nominee services anywhere.

SERVICES WHICH MAY BE PROVIDED IN CONJUNCTION WITH A FIRM OR IN-HOUSE PRACTICE (21.03)

Certain services that fall outside the scope of a solicitor's practice may be provided in conjunction with a firm's or in-house practice. The services are (21.03(1)):

(a) educational and training activities; and

(c) authorship, journalism and publishing.

Such services provided in this way will not be a separate business (21.03(2)).

The 2009 Amendment Rules have removed practice as a qualified notary public from this list.

SERVICES WHICH MAY BE PROVIDED (SUBJECT TO THESE RULES) EITHER THROUGH A FIRM OR IN-HOUSE PRACTICE, OR THROUGH A SEPARATE BUSINESS (21.04)

The 'either way' services are listed in 21.04(1). If the services are provided through a firm or in-house practice, the Code will apply; if the services are provided through a separate business, 21.05 imposes certain safeguards.

The services listed in 21.04 include some of those exceptions to 21.02(2) (see above). The full list is:

(a) alternative dispute resolution;
(b) financial services (except those that cannot form part of a solicitor's practice);
(c) estate agency;
(d) management consultancy;
(e) company secretarial services;
(f) acting as a parliamentary agent;
(g) practising as a lawyer of another jurisdiction;
(h) acting as a bailiff;
(i) acting as nominee, trustee or executor outside England and Wales; or
(j) providing any other business, advisory or agency service which could be provided (subject to these rules) through a firm or in-house practice but is not included in 21.02.

The 2009 Amendment Rules have removed acting as a trade mark agent, patent agent or European patent attorney from this list.

Note 17 gives examples of financial services that cannot form part of a solicitor's practice.

The Code provides a full list of services that can be provided as a separate business and also through a firm or in-house. All of these services will be regulated in one way or another. Where the services are undertaken through a separate business, the conditions (provided by way of safeguards in 21.05) will apply.

SAFEGUARDS IN RELATION TO A SEPARATE BUSINESS (21.05)

Certain safeguards must be put in place, either where a separate business is undertaken as a result of the exceptions in 21.02(2) and/or as a result of the permitted separate businesses listed in 21.04. Safeguards relating to the following matters must be implemented:

- ensuring no breach of rule 1 (Core duties) when making referrals to or accepting referrals from the separate business;
- the way in which the separate business is held out;
- the treatment of paperwork, documents and records of the separate business;

- the use of the practice's client account or other account used to hold money for clients;
- the sharing of premises, office accommodation or reception staff by the separate business with the practice;
- the information that must be given to a client referred to the separate business by the practice;
- additional safeguards regarding conflicts of interest where the separate business is an estate agency.

Note 16 provides detailed guidance on the interpretation of 21.05(2)(a) (the way in which the business is held out) and also provides illustrations of what is permitted and what might lead to a breach.

OTHER GUIDANCE

Notes 11 and 12 provide guidance on executor, trustee and nominee companies and confirm that the services offered by such companies in England and Wales cannot be provided through a separate business. Consequently, such companies must be recognised bodies. Note 6 provides guidance on such companies providing services outside England and Wales.

Notes 14 and 15 deals with service companies and provide that these generally are not separate businesses.

CONCLUSION

While there are no significant changes as a result of the 2009 Amendment Rules, firms who have in the past operated certain separate businesses (notably trade mark and patent agencies and separate practices providing notarial services) will have to ensure that such businesses are now recognised bodies (or operated by recognised sole practitioners).

The rule does apply to e.g. solicitors practising through or employed by an authorised non-SRA firm. For example a solicitor in partnership with or employed by a firm of licensed conveyancers (and thus regulated by the Council for Licensed Conveyancers) would be bound by rule 21 in respect of conveyancing services. The prohibition in rule 21.02(1)(e) would prevent the solicitor's involvement in a separate business providing conveyancing services where the separate business was not a recognised body, a recognised sole practitioner or an authorised non-SRA firm.

CHAPTER 22

Rules 22–25: Waivers, application, interpretation, commencement and repeals

WAIVERS (RULE 22)

Rule 22 permits the SRA to waive in writing the provisions of the rules. However, certain specified rules cannot be waived under these provisions. These are:

(a) rule 1 (Core duties);
(b) rules 3.01 to 3.05 (conflict of interests, excluding provisions relating to alternative dispute resolution, conveyancing and property selling);
(c) rule 4 (Confidentiality and disclosure);
(d) rule 6 (Equality and diversity);
(e) rules 15.01, 15.03, 15.04, 15.18, 15.22, 15.23 and 15.24 (overseas practice provisions which apply provisions that cannot be waived for practice in England and Wales);
(f) rule 18 (Property selling);
(g) rule 22 (Waivers);
(h) rule 23 (Application of these rules); and
(i) rule 24 (Interpretation).

Additional guidance is provided in notes 1–3.

APPLICATION OF THESE RULES (RULE 23)

Rule 23 specifies to whom the rules apply. Chapters 1 to 21 of this Companion provide details of the application of individual rules by reference to the 'Scope' heading.

INTERPRETATION (RULE 24)

Rule 24 defines many of the terms used in the rules. Where appropriate, these definitions have been used in the chapters dealing with the individual rules.

COMMENCEMENT AND REPEALS (RULE 25)

Rule 25 is dealt with in the Introduction to this Companion.

Practice Rules 16D and 16E – Conflict, Confidentiality and Disclosure: Questions, answers and examples

Professional Ethics Unit

June 2006

Note: This Guidance was issued in June 2006 and refers to Practice Rules 16D and 16E. The wording of these practice rules is essentially the same as the wording in rules 3 and 4 of the Solicitors' Code of Conduct 2007. However, you should note that references in the Guidance to the practice rules should now be read as references to the equivalent provisions of rules 3 and 4 of the Code.

INTRODUCTION

This document is intended to provide an introduction to and an overview of the new Practice Rules. Whilst it is fairly detailed, it should still be read in conjunction with the rules themselves and in particular, the Explanatory notes accompanying each new rule which have been issued by the Law Society.

1. Is there a transitional period for the new rule? If not, should I be worrying?

The rule came into immediate effect on the 25 April 2006. However, this does not mean that you have to worry about whether, as a result, you may now be in breach of the new rule. The new rule relaxes the old rule in relation to conflict and disclosure, so provided you were complying with the old provisions, you will not be in breach of the new rule.

2. Why has the rule been changed?

The rule was changed following consultation with the profession, because the old rules in relation to conflict (which are set out in chapter 15 of *The Guide to the Professional Conduct of Solicitors* (1999)), no longer accurately reflect either the position at law (where the courts have increasingly accepted the use of information barriers), or modern business practices.

3. How do the new practice rules differ from the requirements set out in chapters 15 and 16 of *The Guide to the Professional Conduct of Solicitors 1999*?

Many aspects of the new rules and the accompanying guidance will still be familiar. However, the definition of a conflict has changed. It no longer encompasses the situation where the duty of confidentiality you owe to one client conflicts with the duty of disclosure which you owe to another client, as a result of you or your firm being in possession of 'relevant confidential information'. This type of conflict is now dealt with separately and differently in Practice Rule 16E (Confidentiality and Disclosure), which creates a new duty not to put confidentiality at risk by acting.

4. Is it true that a firm may now act in a conflict situation provided there is an information barrier?

No. An information barrier will not 'cure' a conflict. Practice Rule 16E does allow a firm, which would otherwise be in breach of the new duty not to put confidentiality at risk by acting for another client, to continue acting by putting in place an information barrier in certain very limited defined circumstances (see paragraph 34 below). However, this will still not enable you to act for two or more clients where there is a conflict of interests between them (see paragraph 7 below).

5. How do the new rules affect conflicts in conveyancing?

The new rule does not affect either Practice Rule 6 (which sets out the circumstances in which you can act for a seller and a buyer, or a buyer and a lender), or Practice Rule 6A (contract races). You must therefore continue to comply with these rules where relevant.

6. Warning

Both the rules and the Explanatory notes contain important cross references and it is therefore essential that you read the rules and guidance in conjunction with each other. For example, you may not have a conflict under the new definition, but you may still not be able to act because to do so would put confidential information at risk.

A. DETERMINING WHETHER YOU HAVE A CONFLICT OF INTERESTS

7. How is conflict defined under the new rule?

Under the new definition, there will be a conflict of interests if:

- you or your firm owe separate duties to act in the best interests of two or more different clients, and those duties conflict (or there is a significant risk that they will conflict), so that acting in the best interests of one client will result in prejudice to the other client, either in that matter or a related matter; or
- there is a conflict between your interests and those of the client.

8. What is meant by 'related matter'?

Two matters will always be related if they involve the same asset or liability. In other cases, there must be some reasonable degree of relationship between the two matters for a conflict to arise (see notes 2 to 5 of the Explanatory notes).

9. Examples of 'related' matters

(a) You are instructed by X & Co to provide general advice to their HR department in relation to revising the company's staff handbook. Shortly thereafter, your firm is asked to act for one of their former employees, A, in connection with bringing a claim against the company for unfair dismissal. Would your firm have a conflict of interests in agreeing to act for A?

No. The two matters are not directly related. If A succeeds in his claim against the company, that will obviously be prejudicial to the company, but not in relation to the particular retainer you have with the company. Similarly, whatever changes are made to the staff handbook will not have any impact on A's claim against the company.

It is a commercial and reputational decision for you as to whether you want to accept instructions to act against the company. You would also have to consider, as a separate issue, whether the firm would be putting confidentiality at risk through acting for both parties (see paragraph 29 below)

(b) You act for Mr Jones in connection with his divorce and quite separately, for Mr Taylor in connection with his divorce. You have just discovered that Mrs Jones is cohabiting with Mr Taylor (Mr Taylor played no part in the breakdown of Mr & Mrs Jones' marriage). Is there a conflict?

Yes. Although initially the two matters were unrelated, they have become related as a result of Mrs Jones moving in with Mr Taylor, because any financial settlement reached in either matter will clearly have an impact on the other.

(c) You are instructed by A, who has been dismissed for gross misconduct, in bringing a claim for unfair dismissal against his employer, Z & Co. A conflict check reveals that your firm is already acting for Z & Co in defending a claim being brought by another employee for unfair dismissal by reason of redundancy. Would there be a conflict in your firm acting for both clients?

No. The two matters are not related because although both retainers relate to claims for unfair dismissal, the grounds for dismissal in each case are completely unrelated. However, you would have to consider whether your firm has confidential material information from the company, for example with regard to the way in which it deals with claims and if so, whether you would be putting confidentiality at risk by acting.

(d) You have been acting for a wife in connection with matrimonial proceedings which are now concluded. Your client has a costs order against the husband, although these have not yet been paid and you are in correspondence with the husband's solicitors concerning your costs. Your firm has now been approached by the husband who wants your firm to act for him in buying a property. Would your firm have a conflict in agreeing to act?

Yes. Although on the face of it, the two matters are completely unrelated, there is a significant risk that a conflict could arise. If the husband fails to pay the costs, then you would have to advise the wife on what steps to take to enforce the order, which could include applying for a garnishee order on the purchase monies when the husband puts the firm in funds, or taking a charge on the husband's new property. In these circumstances, there is a significant risk that by acting in the best interests of the wife, you would be acting to the prejudice of the husband and your firm should not therefore accept the retainer.

It is not enough just to consider whether the two matters themselves are related. You need to ask yourself whether the fact that your firm acts for both the clients will affect the advice you would give or the steps which you would normally take on behalf of either client and if so, whether this would prejudice the interests of the other client.

10. Exceptions to the conflict rule

There are two exceptions which are intended to have limited and specific application. They must always be used with caution, but recognise that there are certain circumstances when it is beneficial to the clients that the same firm acts. It must be emphasised that this is not for the firm's benefit and clients should not be pushed into agreeing that the firm should act.

11. The 'common interest' exception

The first exception is set out in Practice Rule 16D(3)(a) and is referred to as the 'common interest' exception. It allows you to act for more than one client where the clients have a clear objective in common and any areas of conflict between them are substantially less important to the clients than that common purpose.

To take advantage of this exception:

- all of the clients must have given their informed consent in writing; and
- independently of the client's consent, you must be satisfied, taking account of all of the circumstances, that it is reasonable for you to act despite the conflict or potential conflict.

12. Examples of 'common interest'

(e) You act for a wife in connection with matrimonial proceedings in respect of which the husband is representing himself. There is a consent order whereby the parties have agreed to sell the matrimonial home and have agreed on the distribution of the proceeds of sale. Both parties wish you to act for them in connection with the sale, although there is some disagreement as to what fixtures and fittings should be included in the sale price.

You would be able to act for both parties under the common interest exception, since both parties have a clear common goal. Although there is some dispute concerning fixtures and fittings, this is only a peripheral issue in relation to the main purpose.

(f) You are approached by two partners with a view to one partner buying out the interest of the other partner in their joint business. They want you to act for both of them. Although there is a conflict between their respective interests, can you act for them under the common interest exception?

No. Although both want the same end result, their interests in obtaining that end result are not the same. They are very much in a situation requiring negotiation between them and they cannot therefore be said to have a common interest. In this situation, the transaction serves completely different purposes for each client.

(g) You are asked to act for a mother and a son. The son is taking two loans in connection with his business and it has been agreed that one loan will be secured on the son's flat and the other will be secured on the mother's house. Can you act for both mother and son on the basis that they have a common interest?

No. The two matters are related and there is a conflict because your ability to advise in the best interests of the mother is fettered by your duty to act in the best interests of the son.

Although the mother is willing to enter into the transaction to assist her son, she does not have an interest in the business and cannot therefore be said to share a common purpose with the son. Your firm cannot therefore act for both clients, unless it was possible to limit your retainer with the mother (see paragraph 21 below).

13. What constitutes 'informed consent'?

Before the clients can agree to your acting, you need to explain the situation to each client in such a way that you are satisfied they have clearly understood the issues involved and the risks should you act for both. This includes explaining that if there does come a point when it is no longer reasonable for you to act for all of the clients given their conflicting interests, then you would have to cease acting for one or more of them, with all the delay and extra costs that that will entail.

Obviously, the less sophisticated the client, the more careful you will need to be in ensuring that the client does fully understand the implications. In view of the risk involved, you must be satisfied that each of the clients is of full capacity and that none of the clients is being pressured to give consent by the others.

14. Should I keep a record of my discussions with the client?

Yes. It is most important that you do, because in the event of a subsequent complaint, it will assist you in demonstrating that you complied with the rule.

15. How do I decide whether it is reasonable to act for all the clients?

You need to consider whether the interests of any one client are at risk of being compromised because that client does not have separate representation. This may be because that client is at some disadvantage compared to the other clients, for example:

- because that client has more to lose, or
- because one of the clients is a much stronger character than the other and you cannot be satisfied that the client's wishes are being fully heard; or
- because the other client is in a stronger bargaining position.

In deciding whether it is reasonable to act, you need to take an objective view in the light of everything you know about the transaction and the clients.

Remember, if a complaint is made, the onus will be on you to justify your decision to act. If, therefore, you have concerns this is probably an indication that you should not act for all of the parties.

In certain commercial transactions, it may be common business practice for one firm to act for more than one client and this is certainly something you can take into account in reaching your decision. You can also take into account that it would be disproportionate in terms of both costs and disruption to require the clients to instruct separate solicitors. However, neither of these facts on their own would make it reasonable for you to act.

16. If I am satisfied that the common interest exception applies, how do I deal with the areas of conflict?

The rule is silent on this point, but it will probably depend on the circumstances:

- you could advise the clients jointly on their different options in respect of those areas where there is not agreement, leaving them to come to some agreement whilst you continue to progress those areas where there is agreement

- if they cannot agree, the exception would allow you to refer each client to another colleague in your firm for 'independent' advice on their own position.

Example:

(h) Your firm has acted for a family trust for several years. The beneficiaries, who are all of age, are all clear that they now want to break the trust, although this will affect each beneficiary in different ways. Your firm could act for all of the parties, and could arrange for each beneficiary to be 'independently' advised as to how it would affect them personally by someone else in the firm.

As mentioned above, you would have to keep a very close eye on those areas where there was a conflict and would have to stop acting if the point came when it was no longer tenable to continue acting for all of the clients; for example, because the conflict cannot be resolved and threatens the common purpose, or because the parties cannot be advised even-handedly.

17. The 'competing for the same asset' exception

The second exception is set out in Practice Rule 16D(3)(b) and applies where the clients are competing for the same asset which, if attained by one of them, will make it unattainable to the other. The asset could be a tangible object, but it could also be a business opportunity or a contract.

18. When would it be appropriate to rely on this exception?

This exception is intended to apply to sophisticated clients in specialised areas of practice, where it is common business practice for a firm to act for more than one client in such transactions and the clients are well aware of this. However, you would not be able to rely on this exception to act for more than one client if the clients are in dispute over the asset.

In view of the inherent conflict in this situation, you would have to be extremely cautious in relying on this exception when acting for private clients.

A lot will depend on how readily the situation can be explained to the client and the client understands what is involved.

You would have to vary your duty of disclosure to the clients at the outset and in most cases, since you are likely to acquire material confidential information from both clients, you would only be able to act if you could put in place an information barrier (see paragraphs 29 onwards below).

19. What are the conditions which must be met?

- There must be no other conflict or significant risk of a conflict; and
- all the clients must give their informed written consent (see paragraphs 12 and 13 above); and
- no one individual in your firm must act for, or supervise the fee earner acting for, all of the clients, unless the clients specifically agree; and
- notwithstanding the clients' agreement, it must be reasonable in all the circumstances for you or your firm to act (see paragraph 14 above).

20. If neither of the exceptions apply, is it possible to limit the scope of the retainer, thereby avoiding any conflict?

This is a possibility, either when you are taking on a new client whose interests conflict with those of an existing client, or where you are taking on two clients and there is an area of conflict between them.

However, whether it would be appropriate to do so will depend on the circumstances. For example, it would not be appropriate if one client was in some way disadvantaged compared to the other (this may be as a result of having more to lose, being in a weaker bargaining position and so on). You would need to consider whether you would still be able to act in the client's best interests.

21. Examples

(i) Mrs Smith owns a house. She wants to transfer her property to her son and daughter-in-law who will then take out a mortgage on the property in order to build an extension for Mrs Smith to live in. All three parties want to instruct you. Mrs Smith is adamant that this is what she wants and is happy for you to act on the basis that you do not give any legal advice in respect of the merits of the transaction. Would it be appropriate for you to act for all of the parties if you were to limit Mrs Smith's retainer in this way?

You would be ill advised to act for all of the parties in these circumstances. There is clearly significant potential for a conflict between the interests of the parties and given that Mrs Smith is at a disadvantage in relation to her son and daughter-in-law in terms of her age, what she will be giving up and the extent to which she will be vulnerable if she subsequently fell out with them, she should have an independent solicitor acting for her.

However, if Mrs Smith did take independent advice and still wanted you to go ahead with preparing the transfer documents, this may be a situation where you could act for all the parties by limiting the retainer to preparing the documentation and registering the transfer.

(j) You are asked by a husband and wife to act for them in obtaining a divorce. They have come to an amicable agreement as to the grounds on which the petition will be presented and each has agreed to split the costs equally. They do not want advice on the ancillaries which they have already dealt with. Would it be appropriate for you to act if you were to limit the retainer so that you would not be advising either party?

It is never advisable to act for two parties on opposite sides of a potentially litigious situation, even when limiting the retainer. Although the parties have reached a settlement, it may not be a fair settlement in that one of the parties may not have made full disclosure, or for example, may not have understood that they are entitled to take account of the other's pension rights. Moreover, one party may be taking unfair advantage or exercising undue influence over the other.

If you do limit your retainer, you must obviously make it clear to the client what the limits of the retainer will be and in particular, those areas in which you would not be advising them.

22. What happens if a conflict arises between the interests of two clients, either in the same matter or in related matters, during the course of acting for them?

Your firm cannot continue to act for both parties if a conflict of interests arises. However, you may be able to continue acting for one of the clients provided the duty of confidentiality which you owe to the other client is not put at risk (see paragraph 29 below).

23. When will there be a conflict of interests between me and my client?

The circumstances in which a conflict of interests can arise between you and your client are set out in paragraphs 18–40 of the Explanatory notes. These replace Principles 15.05, 15.06 and 15.07 of *The Guide to the Professional Conduct of Solicitors* (1999), but are basically unchanged.

B. CONFIDENTIALITY AND DISCLOSURE

24. How have the duties of confidentiality and disclosure changed?

The duty of confidentiality you owe to current and former clients, which is now set out in Practice Rule 16E(2), remains unchanged, as do the exceptional circumstances in which confidentiality may be overridden. The guidance in this respect is set out in paragraphs 3 to 20 of the Explanatory notes. The duty you owe to a client to disclose information has been clarified and the rule now makes it clear that where there is a conflict between your duty to disclose and your duty of confidentiality to another client, then it is your duty of confidentiality which will be paramount (although this does not absolve you of your duty to disclose – see paragraph 29 below).

As previously mentioned, the rule also creates a new duty in conduct which is not to put confidential information at risk.

25. What must a solicitor disclose to a client?

As was previously the case, you have a duty to disclose material information to the client, but the rule now makes it clear that this is limited to information which you personally know. You will not therefore be in breach of your duty of disclosure if someone else in your firm has information which would be material to your client's retainer, but which you do not know about.

26. Are there still some exceptions when the duty of disclosure does not arise?

Yes. These are set out in paragraph 21 of the Explanatory notes and are basically unchanged.

27. Does the rule define 'material' information?

No. However, the Explanatory notes make it clear that to be material, the information must be relevant to the specific retainer you have with the client, and must be of more than just passing interest. It must be information which might reasonably be expected to affect the client's decision making in a significant way.

EXAMPLE

(k) You act for a husband in connection with his matrimonial affairs. The husband has threatened his wife on several occasions, as a result of which the wife obtained an order allowing her address not to be disclosed. The wife's solicitors have accidentally disclosed the address, which is a women's refuge, in a copy document they have sent to you. You are aware that your client would like to know the address – do you have an obligation to tell him?

No. Although you know that your client would very much like to know his wife's address, in this example, it is not material information in the sense that it will not affect his decisions or the instructions he gives in relation to his retainer.

28. Does this mean that solicitors should stop doing conflict checks, on the basis that provided the solicitor personally does not have material information, he or she can act?

No. Even though you would not be in breach of your duty of disclosure, you could still be in breach of the duty not to put confidentiality at risk by acting for another party if your firm holds material confidential information (see paragraph 29 below). Your firm is therefore still expected to do a standard conflict check when accepting instructions from a new client. However, for the practicalities involved, see paragraph 30 below.

29. What happens if a solicitor's duty to disclose conflicts with the solicitor's duty of confidentiality?

As a general rule, if you cannot comply with your duty to disclose material information to your client, you must immediately stop acting for the client. There are two exceptional circumstances when it may be possible for you or your firm to continue acting as follows:

Varying the duty of disclosure

In some circumstances, you may be able to vary your duty of disclosure to the client with the client's consent. However, it would be extremely rare that it would be appropriate to do this in a private client matter. One reason for this is that by its very nature, the information is such that it would significantly affect the client's decisions and instructions if the client knew about it and thus, the firm's ability to act in the best interests of the client would be undermined. The other issue is – can you continue to act, bearing in mind the information you hold? Is the information going to affect the way you act? You would also have to consider the professional embarrassment or damage to your reputation if the client subsequently discovered the information you were unable to disclose. If you do vary it, you must explain the implications to the client carefully and must be satisfied that the client had understood what he or she was agreeing to.

Passing the client to another fee earner

Although you personally would have to stop acting, it may occasionally be possible to pass the client on to another fee earner in the firm who is not in possession of the confidential information, thereby enabling the firm to continue acting. To do this, you would first have to explain the reason to the client (without, of course, breaching your duty of confidentiality) and obtain the client's consent. The client would also have to agree to release you from your duty of disclosure up to the point that you stopped acting for the client.

However, for the reasons mentioned above, it will rarely be appropriate to do this in a private client matter. If you do decide to do it, you need to bear in mind that the onus will be on you, in the event of a complaint, to justify your decision to proceed on this basis.

EXAMPLES

(l) You are asked to act for X in buying a property. You previously acted for Y who wanted to buy the same property some months previously, but the transaction fell through following an adverse survey. X has already told you that he does not intend to get his own survey. You have tried to contact Y to obtain his consent to disclose the information to X, but without success.

Clearly you have material information which you cannot disclose, but would it be open to you either:

(i) to continue acting if X agreed to your varying your duty of disclosure, or
(ii) you passed X on to a colleague who was not aware of the material information?

Neither option would be appropriate in these circumstances. That is because the information is fundamental to the ability of the firm to act in the client's best interests, since it goes to the heart of whether or not the client would proceed with the transaction if he knew the information.

(m) You act for X in connection with an employment law issue concerning X's employer. The employer's solicitors have informed you that no other employee has previously complained about the employer's conduct. In seeking advice from a colleague, your colleague has recalled that two years ago, he acted for a client in a dispute with the same employer which was subsequently settled. Whilst the subject matter of that dispute was completely unrelated to your current client's complaint, it is relevant as regards the issue of the employer's credibility. However, you cannot trace the former client to obtain his consent to waiving confidentiality. Again, you clearly have material information, but could you pass the client on to another colleague in these circumstances?

This is one of the rare circumstances where it may be possible to pass the client on. Although the information would clearly assist the client, its non-disclosure would not affect the client's interests. It does not in any way undermine the client's position, in that the information is not central to the client's case and does not affect the ability of the firm to act in the best interests of the client, nor would it affect the advice which the firm gives to the client.

Before seeking the client's consent, however, you would need to consider other factors. For example, if you were responsible for supervising the work of your colleague, it would not be appropriate. Similarly, if your firm or your employment department was very small, you would have to consider such matters as whether you would have to take over the matter if your colleague became ill or went on holiday, or whether there was anyone else for your colleague to consult if required.

30. How does the new duty not to put confidentiality at risk fit in?

Even when you personally do not have material confidential information, you could still be prevented from acting for a client, or continuing to act for a client, if someone else in your firm has confidential information which would be material to your client's retainer.

Practice Rule 16E(4) provides that if you or your firm has confidential information about a client or former client, then you must not risk breaching that confidentiality by acting (or continuing to act) for another client where:

• that client's interests are adverse to the first client's; and
• the confidential information might reasonably be expected to be material.

31. How am I expected to decide this if I don't actually know what the information is?

As mentioned above, when taking on a new client, your firm must still carry out a conflict search, but to avoid any possibility of you acquiring material confidential information, this should not be you. If the search reveals that the firm may have material confidential information about another client or a former client, then the firm will have to evaluate on your behalf whether your firm would be in breach of the duty not to put confidentiality at risk if you were to act for the new client. Where the confidential information is held for an existing client, the person who will make that decision will usually need to consider the information you have and the other client's file and speak to the fee earner acting for the other client to ascertain the risks involved. In doing so, the 'independent' person would have to ensure that no confidential information concerning your client was disclosed to that fee earner, since that may then present that fee earner with difficulties in relation to his or her own duty of disclosure. Your firm will need to consider what procedures it should put in place to deal with these problems. Whoever the firm decides should be the independent person to decide these issues, that person needs to be an experienced legal practitioner, since he or she must not only to be able to ascertain the information which is material, but must also be able to spot whether the firm are likely to acquire material information at some future point in either retainer. If this is a possibility, the independent person will have to keep both matters under review.

In practice, this may well cause difficulties for smaller firms. If so, then those firms may find it easier to decline to act for the new client – i.e. if the conflict check discloses a potential problem, the fee-earner should look at the relevant file and if the firm does hold material confidential information or is likely to do so, should refuse the new instructions.

32. What is meant by 'adverse interest'?

The rule does not give any definition, but the Explanatory notes make it clear that an adverse interest will exist when one client is, or is likely to become, the opposing party in a matter involving negotiations or some form of dispute resolution.

33. What if the confidential information is not material or the clients' interests are not adverse?

If the information is material but the clients' interests are not adverse, or vice versa, then the rule will not apply and your firm (or you, if you do not know what the material information is) will be able to act for the client, provided the information is protected.

What steps your firm takes to protect the information will be a matter for your firm and will depend on the circumstances. It is usually much easier to protect the confidentiality of former clients than existing clients. This is particularly so, for example, where both clients' matters are being dealt with in the same office and there is a shared use of resources, such as secretarial staff, computers and fax machines. If you cannot be absolutely sure that confidential information will not inadvertently be disclosed, you should not act or continue to act for the client to whom the information is material.

34. Does the client have to be told in these circumstances that the firm has material confidential information which cannot be disclosed?

Although the rule does not require it, as a matter of good practice, the client should usually be told so that the client has an opportunity to consider whether he or she would rather go elsewhere. However, a lot will depend on the nature of the material confidential information and the effect it would have on the client if it were subsequently to become known that your firm was in possession of the information whilst acting for this client. Your firm will need to consider the sensitivities involved, particularly in a private client matter. If the information would materially affect the way in which you would act for the client, or if it undermines your ability to act in the client's best interests, then you should not act or, if you are already acting, you should cease acting for the client. As discussed in paragraph 30, this decision would have to be made on your behalf by the firm.

For example, suppose in Example (l) above, someone other than you acted for the previous buyer. If this had shown up in the conflict check, the firm would have to decide, on your behalf, whether it was appropriate for you to take on the new client. In this case, it would not be since the nature of the information clearly means that the firm could not act in the best interests of the client.

35. In what circumstances can a solicitor use an information barrier?

Despite the duty not to put confidentiality at risk by acting, there are two exceptions set out in Practice Rule 16E(5) and (6) which allow your firm or you (if you do not know what the confidential information is) to act or to continue acting for the client to whom the confidential information is material. Both involve protecting the confidential information by means of an information barrier, but the conditions attached to each exception differ. However, it must be stressed that generally speaking, the use of information barriers is only appropriate where the clients are sophisticated users of legal services and capable of fully appreciating the risks. Further, this is a device to be used for the clients' benefit because it is something they want and not purely because it enables the firm to accept new instructions.

N.B. For the purpose of explaining this part of the rule, 'client A' is used to refer to the client to whom the information is material, and 'client Z' is used to refer to the client (who may be an existing or former client) to whom the firm owes a duty of confidentiality.

36. When does the first exception apply?

The first exception is where client Z gives informed consent to your acting or continuing to act. Before proceeding, you must be satisfied that:

- both clients understand the relevant issues and client A, who may be an existing client or a new one, has also given informed consent; and
- independently of both clients' consent, it is reasonable in all the circumstances for you to act

37. What is the second exception?

The second exception only applies when you are already acting for client A when it becomes clear that the firm has material confidential information, but either client Z refuses consent or it is not possible to seek consent. This could be, for example, because the client cannot be contacted, or because making the request would itself breach client A's confidentiality. In this case, you must be satisfied that:

- client A understands that your firm holds, or might hold, material information which cannot be disclosed; and
- the safeguards to protect the confidential information comply with the requirements at law at that time; and
- it is reasonable in all the circumstances for you to continue acting on this basis.

However, you must never underestimate the severity of the protections required by the law to put in place an information barrier without A's consent. These will be beyond the capability of most firms. Whatever the reason for proceeding without Z's consent, client Z should, as a general rule, be told that you have put an information barrier in place as soon as you are able and you should explain the steps you have taken to protect the information. There may however be circumstances when it might be appropriate to wait or, indeed, where it is impossible to inform the client (see paragraph 38 of the Explanatory notes).

38. If client Z has refused consent and we decide to proceed on the above basis, surely he is likely to complain?

Yes. Before deciding to proceed, you obviously need to consider Z's value as a client to the firm and whether it makes good business sense to proceed with the information barrier in the face of the client's refusal, even if you feel there is no good reason for that refusal.

You also need to consider the possibility of the client taking action at law to prevent you from continuing to act for your other client. In this respect, if you do proceed, not only must you be absolutely sure that your information barrier complies with the law, but also that you do not have a conflict of interests. Remember, an information barrier cannot be used to cure a conflict. If therefore, you were currently acting for Z, you would have to be satisfied that Z and A's matters were not related.

39. What information should be given to the clients when seeking their consent?

You need to explain to both clients what the potential risks are if you act. This includes explaining that if it became impossible to comply with any of the terms, the firm may have to cease acting. Similarly, where you are proceeding without the consent of client Z, it should be explained to client A that Z could make an application to the court to prevent the firm acting for A. The clients' consent should not be sought if there is a particular risk of prejudicing the position of either of them.

40. Should the clients' consent be obtained in writing?

Ideally yes, although the rule itself does not require it. It is also advisable to confirm in writing to the respective clients all of the advice and information given to them in case this is subsequently called into question.

41. How should the firm go about setting up an information barrier?

If you are acting with the informed consent of client Z, the arrangements you make should be discussed and agreed with that client, but they would normally be expected to include some or all of paragraph 44(a) to (f) of the Explanatory notes, in addition to considering which of the other steps listed may be appropriate.

If you are acting without consent, the standard of the protection is much higher and you should comply with most, but preferably all, of the requirements in paragraph 44(a) to (n).

42. Is it expected that information barriers will be commonly used by all practices?

No. For one thing, you will have to consider very carefully in each case whether you have been able to disclose sufficient information for the client's consent to be given on an informed basis. The duty of confidentiality you owe to the other client will usually make this very difficult. For this reason, it will generally only be very sophisticated clients, such as a company with its own in-house department, who will have the experience and ability to fully understand the implications and assess the risks.

Secondly, the information barrier must be effective to avoid any risk of inadvertent disclosure. The smaller your firm, the harder in practice this is likely to be. Although the rule does not specify that there must be a geographical separation for an effective information barrier to be put in place, the burden on you to demonstrate that there is an effective barrier will be much harder to discharge if, for example, the matters are being dealt with in one office with no obvious separation (e.g. such as different floors of the same office). Even if this is not a problem, if you do not have sufficient fee earners, you are unlikely to be in a position to put in place an effective information barrier. The additional cost of putting in place an information barrier is another factor which may deter firms.

43. If I am already acting for client A when the issue of material confidential information arises, am I obliged to erect an information barrier if A insists?

No. It is a decision for your firm as to whether you continue acting by means of an information barrier, or whether you cease acting.

44. What happens if a partner or fee earner moves firms and the respective firms act on opposite sides of a matter?

The solicitor moving firms could not personally act for the client in the new firm if that solicitor had material confidential information concerning the client of his former firm. If the clients' interests were not adverse, the new firm could continue acting but the solicitor would have to ensure that the former client's confidentiality was protected. If the parties' interests were adverse, then the firm would only be able to continue acting for their client if an information barrier could be put in place to protect the information of the other party in accordance with 16E(5) or (6).

EXAMPLE

(n) Firm A acts for the husband in connection with matrimonial proceedings in which the wife is represented by firm B. The parties have agreed on a consent order although there are still some pension issues which need to be resolved. The fee earner in firm A is now moving to firm B, although she will not have any involvement in the wife's retainer. Can firm B continue to act?

Although the fee earner from firm A will have no further involvement in the matter, she will have material confidential information. Since the parties' interests are adverse, the firm will be putting confidentiality at risk through continuing to act unless it can protect the other party's information by putting an information barrier in place in accordance with 16E(5) or (6). Given that the parties are involved in litigation, the firm would have to consider carefully the risks in proceeding if the husband was not prepared to give consent.

45. What happens when two firms amalgamate?

If, following the amalgamation, the new firm has a conflict of interests between two clients, then the firm must cease acting for both clients, unless it can properly continue to act for one of the clients on the basis that any material confidential information it holds in respect of the other client can be protected by means of an information barrier. However, the firm would have to consider the legal position very carefully before proceeding on this basis if the other client was not prepared to give consent.

In other cases where there is no conflict, but the new firm has acquired material confidential information from a current or former client, the new firm would have to cease acting for the client to whom the information is material and the clients' interests are adverse unless again, the information can be protected by means of an information barrier.

C. FURTHER EXAMPLES

(o) Firm A act for a husband in connection with his divorce and Firm B are acting for the wife in connection with those proceedings. Firm C are acting for both husband and wife in the sale of the matrimonial home. Firm A has now discovered that they are also acting for the buyer. Can they continue to act for both parties?

The first point to decide is whether Firm A has a conflict of interests. Although the matters are related, on the face of it, both the buyer and the husband want the same thing. There would not necessarily be a conflict in acting for both parties therefore, unless, for example, the husband had told his solicitor that he did not want the sale to go through, or he wanted to delay it as long as possible. If that was the case, the firm could not act in the best interests of both clients. Since neither of the exceptions would apply in this instance, the firm would have to cease acting.

(p) You act for a wife in connection with divorce proceedings. There is a consent order under the terms of which the jointly owned matrimonial home is to be transferred to the wife in return for a small capital payment to the husband and the wife must use her best endeavours to have the husband released from the terms of the mortgage. The wife has now agreed with her son that she will continue to live in the property, but the property should be transferred to the son who will take out his own mortgage on the property and pay the father the sum due to him with the existing mortgage being redeemed. The wife and son want you to act for both of them in achieving this – can you act?

No, because there is a conflict between the interests of the wife and her son. Although the parties want the same result, their interests in obtaining that result are not the same and this is not therefore a situation where the 'common interest' exception would apply. In view of the obvious disadvantages to the wife, this is not a case where it would be advisable to proceed on the basis of a limited retainer.

(q) Your firm has been asked to act for Mr and Mrs Smith in connection with care proceedings. Mr Smith has been charged with indecent assault and is awaiting trial, although your firm is not instructed in these matters. Mr Smith is intending to plead not guilty and Mrs Smith tells you that she believes her husband is innocent. Can the firm agree to act for both parents?

No. There is likely to be a conflict between the two clients. Even though Mrs Smith believes her husband to be innocent, the criminal charges against him means that the advice which your firm should be giving her as regards her best chance of succeeding in the care proceedings is fettered by the fact that you also have a duty to act in his best interests. The firm cannot therefore act for both parties.

(r) You are normally employed by J. Bloggs & Co, but for the past three months have been on secondment to a client company, working in their legal department. In this guise, you have been instructed by the company to negotiate a know-how agreement with X, who is also a client of your firm and for whom you have acted in the past. Do you have a problem in doing the work for the company?

It depends. The first point to consider is whether you have confidential information concerning X which is material to this particular matter. If you do, then the continuing duty of confidentiality you owe X in respect of that information cannot be reconciled with the duty of disclosure you owe the company and you would therefore have to cease acting on this matter, unless you can agree with the company to vary your duty of disclosure. It would only be reasonable to do this provided the nature of the information does not undermine your ability to act in the best interests of the company.

If you do not have material confidential information, then you can act, but you need to keep the matter under review.

When returning to your firm, you will need to consider whether you have any confidential information as a result of the secondment which is material to another client of your firm. If you do, the duty of confidentiality you owe the company means that you cannot disclose the information either to clients of the firm or to other fee earners within the firm and you would not therefore be able to act for those clients. In addition, if the interests of the clients were adverse (see paragraphs 29 and 31 above), you and your firm would have to put in place safeguards in accordance with 16E(5) or (6) to ensure that the information is protected. If the interests of the clients are not adverse, you could still not act for the other client in view of your duty of disclosure, but your firm may be able to do so, depending on the nature of the information.

Index